SAMS Teach Yourself Microsoft® SharePoint™ 2003 in 10 Minutes

Colin Spence and
Michael Noel

800 East 96th Street, Indianapolis, Indiana, 46240 USA

Sams Teach Yourself Microsoft® SharePoint 2003 in 10 Minutes

International Standard Book Number: 0-672-32723-6

Library of Congress Catalog Card Number: 2004096712

Printed in the United States of America

First Printing: December, 2004

07 06 05 4

Trademarks

Warning and Disclaimer

Bulk Sales

Sams Publishing offers excellent discounts on this book when ordered in quantity for bulk purchases or special sales. For more information, please contact

U.S. Corporate and Government Sales
1-800-382-3419
corpsales@pearsontechgroup.com

For sales outside of the U.S., please contact

International Sales
international@pearsoned.com

Associate Publisher
Michael Stephens

Acquisitions Editor
Neil Rowe

Development Editor
Songlin Qiu

Managing Editor
Charlotte Clapp

Project Editor
George E. Nedeff

Copy Editor
Bart Reed

Proofreader
Tracy Donhardt

Technical Editor
Peter Pham

Publishing Coordinator
Cindy Teeters

Interior Designer
Gary Adair

Cover Designer
Aren Howell

Page Layout
Bronkella Publishing

Contents

PART II Using the Standard Libraries and Lists

PART III Customizing Standard Libraries and Lists

Part IV Using Office 2003 Products with SharePoint

Part V SharePoint Site Administration Basics

About the Authors

Colin Spence is a Partner at Convergent Computing, and performs in the role of a Consultant, Project Manager, and Technical Writer for the organization. He focuses on the design, implementation, and support of Microsoft-based technology solutions, with a current focus on Microsoft SharePoint technologies. Colin has contributed to *Microsoft Windows Server 2003 Unleashed*, *Microsoft Exchange Server 2003 Unleashed*, and was a co-author on *Microsoft SharePoint 2003 Unleashed* by Sams Publishing.

Michael Noel (MCSE+I, MCSA) has significant experience in the computer industry and has been working with the latest in SharePoint, Windows, Exchange, and Security technologies since the early stages of the products. Michael is the coauthor of *SharePoint 2003 Unleashed*, *Windows Server 2003 Unleashed*, and *Exchange Server 2003 Unleashed* by Sams Publishing and is currently working on authoring his next title, *ISA Server 2004 Unleashed*. Currently a Senior Consultant at Convergent Computing in the San Francisco Bay area, Michael brings a wealth of hands-on knowledge and experience to his writing and public-speaking engagements.

Dedications

I would like to dedicate this book to my loving and supporting wife, Nancy. Thanks for your patience and understanding while this project came together.

—Colin

This book is dedicated to my grandparents, Phyllis and George Noel. The lives you have led have been an inspiration to me.

—Michael

We Want to Hear from You!

As the reader of this book, *you* are our most important critic and commentator. We value your opinion and want to know what we're doing right, what we could do better, what areas you'd like to see us publish in, and any other words of wisdom you're willing to pass our way.

As an associate publisher for Sams Publishing, I welcome your comments. You can email or write me directly to let me know what you did or didn't like about this book—as well as what we can do to make our books better.

Please note that I cannot help you with technical problems related to the topic of this book. We do have a User Services group, however, where I will forward specific technical questions related to the book.

When you write, please be sure to include this book's title and author as well as your name, email address, and phone number. I will carefully review your comments and share them with the author and editors who worked on the book.

Email: feedback@samspublishing.com

Mail: Michael Stephens
Associate Publisher
Sams Publishing
800 East 96th Street
Indianapolis, IN 46240 USA

For more information about this book or another Sams Publishing title, visit our website at www.samspublishing.com. Type the ISBN (0672327236) or the title of a book in the Search field to find the page you're looking for.

Introduction

The primary goal of the book is to provide SharePoint users with a series of short lessons, each designed to take roughly 10 minutes to read, that provide information and examples of the processes that are most important for SharePoint users. Our experiences in the field with organizations of many different sizes (10 users to thousands of users) that use SharePoint helped us determine information that would be the most useful to the broadest audience. We also used feedback from end-user and Site Administrator training classes as well as feedback from public speaking engagements to further fine-tune the lessons.

Who Is This Book For?

This book targets two specific audiences:

- Users who have had minimal or no exposure to SharePoint—the "end user"
- Individuals who are tasked with maintaining site collections—the "Site Administrator"

In our experience, we have found that many people tasked to be Site Administrators do not have a significant technology background or training, so the early lessons may also be useful to them. Also, as end users get more sophisticated and familiar with SharePoint's features, they can benefit from the information contained in the latter lessons of the book.

What Does this Book Cover?

The information and examples provided in this book apply to Windows SharePoint Services or SharePoint Portal Server 2003 with SP1 applied. Previous versions of SharePoint—SharePoint Team Services and SharePoint Portal Server 2001—are not covered in this book. The examples in this book were performed on a Windows XP Workstation with Internet Explorer version 6.0. Although other operating systems and

Internet browsers can be used to access SharePoint 2003 sites, they may provide slightly different levels of functionality.

Although the lessons and examples given in this book are valid for end users and Site Administrators of SharePoint Portal Server 2003, the portal-level features of SharePoint Portal Server 2003 are not covered in this book.

Goals for Parts I–IV

Parts I–IV of this book are written for end users who are new to the world of SharePoint or who have gaps in their knowledge that they would like to fill. These parts use a fictitious site named "ProServices" to provide examples of the topics being covered that seek to meet the needs of the average end user. Ideally these lessons will be read in order because the skills build upon each other, and jumping between lessons for a new user may not be as effective. More experienced SharePoint end users should be more comfortable browsing to find topics of specific interest.

If you want to follow the steps in the examples, it is recommended that you use a standard blank Team Site rather than a production site. If you don't have a blank Team Site available, request the Site Administrator create one for you and give you Contributor or Administrator rights. If you want to work through Parts V–VII, you will need Administrator rights to the site.

Your site will not look exactly like the one shown in the figures in this book—it contains additional sample documents and data entries that your site will not contain.

> **TIP** If you find yourself unable to complete a series of steps outlined in Lessons 1–14, check with your Site Administrator to see what might be causing the problem. It will generally be due to a limitation in your rights on the site.

Goals for Parts V–VII

Parts V–VII of this book are geared toward those individuals who have been given the responsibility to administer a Windows SharePoint Services site. The role of the Site Administrator is defined, and the most common tasks you will need to perform as a Site Administrator are detailed in the lessons in this section.

This section of the book only applies to individuals who are given full Site Administrator rights to a site because the majority of all the procedures described require those rights. It is meant to be a guide for you if you are tasked with the creation and customization of a new site for your team or project.

The lessons in Parts V–VII are meant to be read sequentially, but you can also reference them individually, because they are all self-supporting and none of the tasks require any prerequisite steps from earlier lessons. In this way, you can use this portion of the book as a reference guide if you need to look back to recall how to perform a specific task.

Conventions Used in This Book

NOTE A note presents interesting pieces of information related to the surrounding discussion.

TIP A tip offers advice or teaches you an easier way to do something.

CAUTION A caution advises you about potential pitfalls you should avoid or take into account.

The ➥ character signifies that the author means for multiple lines of code to appear on the same line.

Lesson 1

Introduction to SharePoint 2003

In this lesson you'll get an overview of what SharePoint is and what it is designed to do.

Windows SharePoint Services Versus SharePoint Portal Server 2003

The SharePoint family is composed of two products: Windows SharePoint Services and SharePoint Portal Server 2003. Windows SharePoint Services is the basic "engine" that provides document management and collaboration features, whereas SharePoint Portal Server 2003 adds additional portal functionality that is useful to larger organizations. Windows SharePoint Services is a free download that can be added to a Windows Server 2003 server, whereas SharePoint Portal Server 2003 must be purchased and licensed as a separate product.

NOTE SharePoint Team Services and SharePoint Portal Server 2001 are the previous versions of the products. If you are using them, this book won't apply because the interfaces and features are different.

Figure 1.1 provides an illustration of Windows SharePoint Services, as composed of a group of site collections of different sizes, and of SharePoint Portal Server 2003 consisting of areas, site collections, and personal sites. As this picture illustrates, the portal provides a number of different elements, in a structured fashion, whereas Windows SharePoint

Services is limited to site collections. This being said, Windows SharePoint Services still offers a wealth of document management and collaboration features, and it's used by many organizations getting started on the knowledge management path.

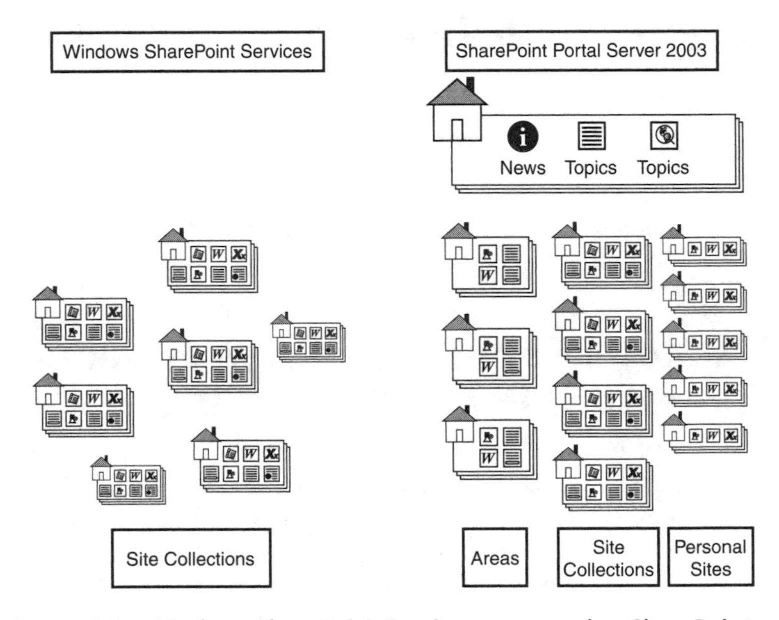

FIGURE 1.1 Windows SharePoint Services compared to SharePoint Portal Server 2003.

You'll note in the image that each site collection in Windows SharePoint Services contains a house graphic, which represents the home page for that site collection, and several other icons representing the types of information that can be accessed from that home page. Documents that can be accessed from the home page include Microsoft documents (such as Project, Word, Excel, and PowerPoint documents), other non-Microsoft documents stored in document libraries (such a PDF files), as well as pictures (such as TIF, JPG, and GIF files), lists, and forms. These are typically made available through Web Parts, which will be discussed in more detail throughout the book.

Other information, such as hyperlinks (or URL links), can be accessed from the site home page. What's more, other websites can be displayed in a window within the site. Suffice it to say at this point that a SharePoint site home page can provide access to a vast array of information.

NOTE Most portal and Site Administrators will limit the types of files that can be uploaded to a SharePoint site. This helps them enforce company standards on supported file types, and it also helps them keep file types that are more likely to have viruses embedded in them out of the SharePoint environment.

There are also several pages shown for each site collection in the image, because a site can have subsites (some of which are called *workspaces*) beneath it. Although there is no real limit to how "deep" a site collection can go, in most environments the Site Administrators will strive to control the complexity of the overall structure, because navigating between the different sites can get confusing and increase the amount of time it takes users to find the information they are looking for.

In this book we'll assume that the user is working with Windows SharePoint Services, so we'll concentrate on the features and functionality provided by Windows SharePoint Services. There may well be a SharePoint Portal Server 2003 environment configured above and beyond the Windows SharePoint Services sites, but don't worry because the skills you'll learn in this book will also apply to the portal. For example, the areas in a portal will contain lists and libraries that the site collections contain. Personal sites on the portal also contain the same lists and document libraries and can be customized in the same way they can in Windows SharePoint Services sites. So once you have worked through the lessons in this book, you will be comfortable with portal areas and personal sites as well.

Portals are created by organizations with more extensive document management and collaboration needs, by organizations that want the added features of areas and personal sites (as well as enhanced search capabilities), and for access to some of the additional high-end features that SharePoint Portal Server 2003 offers. These include the ability to create multiple portals (some for internal use, and perhaps some for external customers to use) and link them together, and the ability to offer single sign-on services (so a user can access a number of business applications with one login). SharePoint Portal Server 2003 also offers enhanced management tools designed to handle very large and complex structures with hundreds or even thousands of sites and site collections.

How Do I Access a SharePoint Site?

Accessing a SharePoint site can be done in a number of ways, but the most standard way is to simply use your browser—either Microsoft Internet Explorer (version 5.01 or later, with latest service packs for security reasons) or Netscape Navigator 6.2 or later. If you are using a Macintosh computer, you can use Internet Explorer 5.2 for Mac OS X, plus the latest service packs, or Netscape Navigator 6.2 for the Mac.

As you will find out later in the book, you can access a SharePoint site by clicking a hyperlink that someone sends you in an email or by saving a document directly to the site from within Word or Excel or another application. For general use, however, most people simply open their browser and type in the URL of the SharePoint site (such as http://*servername/sitename* or http://*portal.domain.com/sitename*). Lesson 2, "Accessing SharePoint Sites," will cover additional navigation skills that will save you time and effort when working with SharePoint sites.

Basic Features of a SharePoint Site

Figure 1.2 shows a standard SharePoint site that has just been created using the Team Site template. It does not yet have any content uploaded to it or customizations made to its look and feel. As any SharePoint site is customized and fine-tuned by the Site Administrator, it will change in appearance. Therefore, it is very possible that the sites you see in your organization may appear quite different, may have graphics and logos applied, as well as more complex links and color schemes. The main components, however, as outlined here, should be the same.

Presented within the IE frame, the site provides the following main components:

1. **The address bar**—This component contains the URL of the site (https://sp.cco.com/sites/ProServices/default.aspx), the last part of which (default.aspx) is the actual name of the page that is

being displayed. It may be helpful to think of the page being displayed as a document that simply has some hyperlinks and other elements included in it, much like a Word document that has some tables, graphics, and hyperlinks inserted in it.

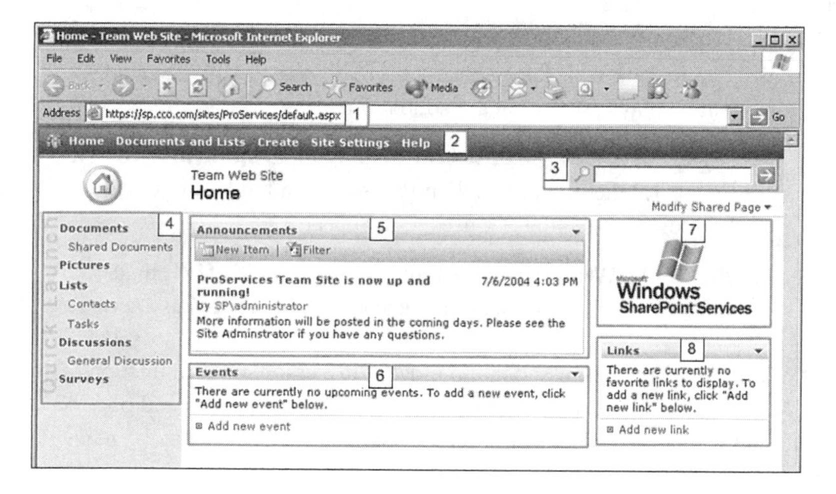

FIGURE 1.2 SharePoint team site.

2. **The navigation bar**—This shaded component lines the top of the page and includes links to other pages useful for users of the site: Home, Documents and Lists, Create, Site Settings, and Help. In this case, the page displayed is the home page of the site collection ProServices, so clicking the Home link in the navigation bar will simply refresh the page. However, the ability to return to the home page can be very helpful if you find yourself "lost" within the site and want to quickly return to familiar territory.

3. **The search bar**—This component should look familiar because search bars appear on many websites. It allows you to search for whole words that appear in documents either stored in the site or contained in lists.

4. **The Quick Launch bar**—This component is shown along the left side of the screen and provides a table of contents view of the different libraries and lists contained within the site. Note that the Quick Launch bar might *not* show every available list or

library because the Site Administrator can determine which Web Parts it displays.

5. **The Announcements Web Part**—This Web Part, as the title suggests, displays announcements that are meant for users of the site to see on the home page.
6. **The Events Web Part**—This Web Part is essentially a calendar that displays events that are added to it.
7. **A view of a Web Part used for displaying graphic images**—In Figure 1.2 the title of this Web Part has been hidden so just the Windows SharePoint Services logo appears.
8. **The Links Web Part**—The Links Web Part holds URL links to show users related or helpful websites and pages for easy access.

Web Parts will be discussed in more detail in Lesson 4, "Introduction to Web Parts," as these are key components to SharePoint sites and provide the functionality of document libraries and lists, as well as having many other functions.

How Organizations Use SharePoint

SharePoint is designed to help organizations manage their documents and files, as well as to enable users to collaborate with one another. Although every organization with a network already has tools in place (file shares, shared directories, intranets) to store files and share information, SharePoint offers more powerful and flexible tools than the average company had previously. For example, SharePoint allows the creation of document libraries that can store not only the documents uploaded to the library, but also information about the documents (called *metadata*) in special columns that can be added to the libraries. Access to this information can be quite rigidly controlled so that some users can only read the documents whereas others can read and modify them. The libraries can be configured to store previous versions of the documents as well, so a history of changes can be kept.

In terms of collaboration, most companies rely on email to share files and use face-to-face meetings when multiple people need to be involved in a conversation. Although emailing a document to a group of people is one way to share it, most users agree it is not the most efficient way to share information, and things can get confusing when more than one current document is floating around. SharePoint sites provide an alternative, where specific network users can be invited to the site to access the latest version of the document, track document versions, add comments to documents, and use discussion boards to share ideas.

Following is a short list of some common uses for SharePoint sites:

- A departmental site to provide a central place to store files, contacts, announcements, and other departmental information
- A project site to allow a team of people to collaborate and share documents within the site, which is managed by a designated project manager
- An event site created for an important meeting or gathering to provide directions, an agenda, a menu, a list of attendees, and other information
- A management site to collect information from other sites or external sources and enhance a manager's ability to keep an eye on the many sources of information

A variety of other companies offer similar knowledge management software, but Microsoft's SharePoint offers several key advantages:

- It integrates with the Windows Server 2003 software.
- It integrates with the Microsoft Office 2003 family.
- It has very competitive pricing.
- It's relatively easy to set up for the IT staff.
- It's relatively easy to learn and use for knowledge workers and end users.

The bulleted point pertaining to integration with the Office 2003 family bears some explanation. Office 2003 is not required, but it does add a number of powerful features when used with SharePoint. Although some integration is provided by previous versions of Office, Office 2003 integrates the most completely, providing additional functionality. Lesson 13, "Using Word with SharePoint," and Lesson 14, "Using Excel with SharePoint," discuss some of the benefits of using Word 2003 and Excel

2003 with SharePoint. As shown in Figure 1.3, when a document stored in a SharePoint document library is opened for editing, the Shared Workspace task pane is available, and it displays information about the site that houses the document. In this figure the Members tab is active, and it shows that several other individuals have access to this same document. The other tabs can provide information about tasks assigned to the user from SharePoint, other documents in the same library, links in the site, and metadata connected to the document.

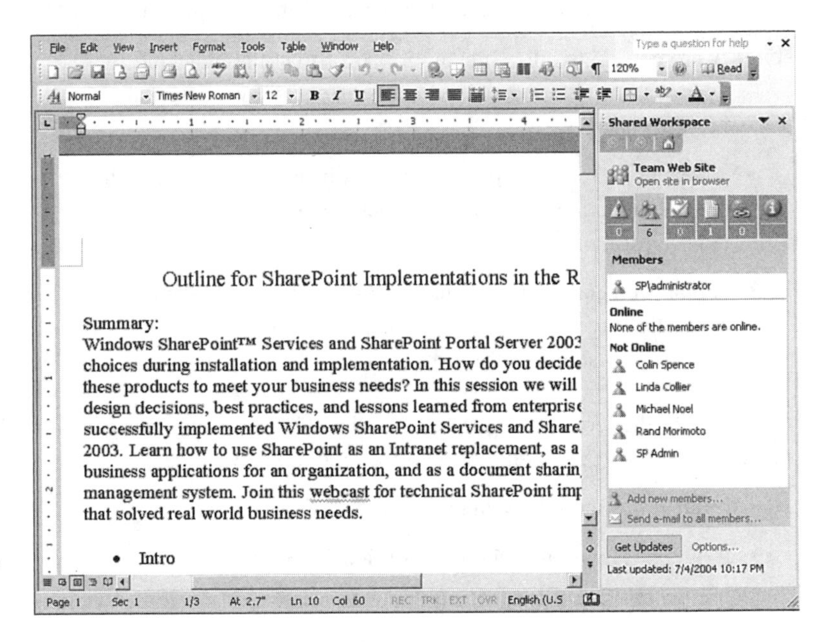

FIGURE 1.3 Word 2003 Shared Workspace task pane.

Summary

This lesson provided a brief overview and defined SharePoint as well as demonstrated the difference between Windows SharePoint Services and SharePoint Portal Server 2003. An introduction on how to access a SharePoint site was given. An overview of the main components of a SharePoint site, and some sample uses for SharePoint sites were also provided. Each of these topics will be explored in more detail in the lessons that follow.

Lesson 2

Accessing SharePoint Sites

In this lesson you will learn how to effectively use Internet Explorer 6.0 to access SharePoint sites and how to use My Network Places.

Internet Explorer Fundamentals

Most users are familiar with how to use Internet Explorer (IE) to access sites on the Internet, and the same basic skills are required to access SharePoint sites. We will explore some of the more advanced capabilities of IE in this lesson, because an understanding of how IE can be customized and configured will enhance your efficiency in navigating through SharePoint sites.

SharePoint supports access from other browsers, but IE 6.0 (or newer) for Windows is recommended because using older versions of IE or Netscape Navigator will result in some loss of functionality. The following browsers are supported, some with limitations:

- Internet Explorer 5.01 SP3, 5.5x, and 6.x for Windows
- Navigator 6.2+ for Windows
- Navigator 6.2 for Unix
- Navigator 6.2 for Macintosh
- Internet Explorer 5.2 for Macintosh

Figure 2.1 shows a standard IE 6.0 screen, displaying the ProServices site referenced in Lesson 1, "Introduction to SharePoint 2003."

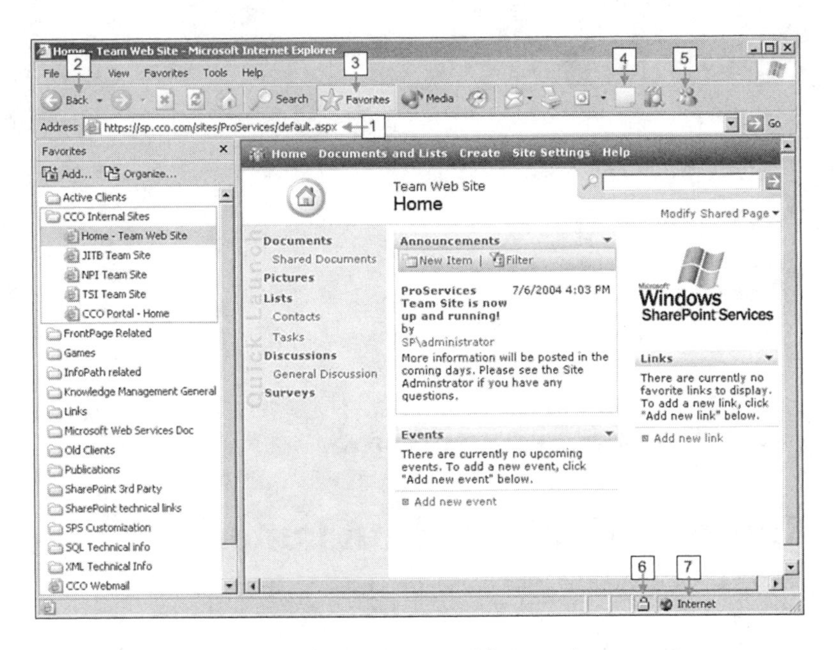

FIGURE 2.1 Internet Explorer screen with Favorites panel.

The numbers in this figure point out several key features in Internet Explorer 6.0:

1. The address bar, as most people know, is where you type in the URL address to access a specific website. After the address has been entered, you can either press the Enter key or click the green arrow located to the right of the address bar. In this case, note that the address starts with *https* instead of the normal *http*. The *s* indicates that the connectivity is taking place using SSL (Secure Sockets Layer), which enhances the security of the connection by encrypting the data.

2. Although it may seem fairly obvious, the Back button is extremely useful, even for the most experienced users. Using SharePoint can be akin to flipping from one page in a book to another, and then another, and then another. It can become hard to remember which page you were on a few minutes ago. Clicking the Back button, or pressing the Backspace key, allows you to retrace your steps to help you find a previous page. Note

that pressing the Backspace key when text is highlighted in a text box will most likely delete it, so there are times when it is better to use the actual Back button in the toolbar.

3. Most users are experienced with favorites, and in Figure 2.1 the Favorites button is selected, resulting in the display of the favorites along the left side of the screen. In this figure, the ProServices site is listed as "Home – Team Web Site" in the Favorites panel on the left, because that is the title that was given to the home page. In this case, the title isn't very informative, so a title such as "Home – ProServices Site" would be better.

4. The Discuss button can be selected to add Web discussion notes to the SharePoint page. Most people aren't familiar with this tool, and in general it is rarely used. If you do add discussions to a page, another viewer of the site would need to click the Discuss button to see them, so he or she would have to know to look for them. A general recommendation is to *not* use this feature unless you have a specific need for it—for example, if you are a Web designer commenting on the layout of a page.

5. The Messenger feature will only work if instant messaging is configured on the network.

6. This area indicates whether the site being visited is secure. In this case, because SSL is being used, the closed padlock icon appears.

7. This area labels the zone that the current site is a member of (in this case, the Internet zone). Zones will be discussed later in this lesson in more detail.

TIP The row of buttons beneath the standard menu area is called the *toolbar*. If it is not displayed in IE, you can display it by selecting **View, Toolbars, Standard Buttons.** Likewise, if the address bar is not displaying, you can find it in the same place.

Understanding the Internet Options

Hidden under the Tools menu in IE 6.0 is the Internet Options tool. Within the Internet Options dialog box is an extensive set of tools that affects how IE behaves relative to SharePoint sites. Although all the tabs in the Internet Options dialog box have extensive features, we will concentrate on just the Security and Advanced tabs in the section.

CAUTION Before changing any of the settings in the Internet Options dialog box, check with your Site Administrator or friendly help desk person to see whether it's okay to do so. Some organizations lock down the settings in IE, and you won't be able to change any settings, whereas others have standards and guidelines they follow and simply discourage any changes. Take care when making changes within any of the tabs!

Figure 2.2 shows the Security tab within the Internet Options dialog box and the four Web content zones that IE uses to categorize different types of sites. You can add sites to any zone other than the Internet zone by highlighting the zone and clicking the Sites button, then typing in the address in the **Add this Web site to the zone** cell, and then clicking Add. Here are brief definitions of the zones:

- **The Internet zone**—This zone contains all websites that haven't been added to other zones. The default security level is High for the Internet zone.
- **The Local Intranet zone**—This zone contains all websites that are considered to be part of the company's intranet. The default security level to this zone is Medium-Low.
- **The Trusted sites zone**—This zone contains the websites that you trust not to damage your computer or data. The default security setting to this zone is Low.

- **The Restricted sites zone**—This zone contain websites that you feel could potentially damage your computer or data. The default security setting to this zone is High.

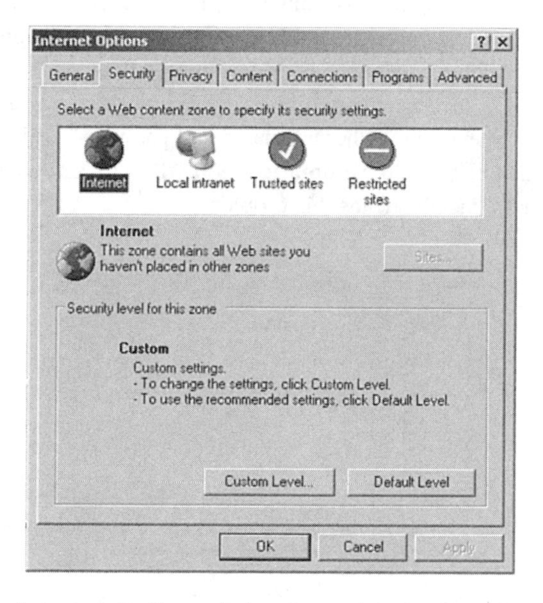

FIGURE 2.2 Internet Options dialog box with the Security tab active.

TIP Adding your SharePoint site or sites to the Trusted Sites zone is a recommended best practice in most cases. Because this site is run and managed by the organization you work for, it is generally a safe bet to trust the site and subsites. Note also that the default authentication is to use **Automatic logon with current username and password**, which can eliminate the need to enter in your username and password every time you access the SharePoint site or open a document stored in a document library if you are on the local network of your company. From a home or remote computer accessing the SharePoint site over the Internet, you will still be prompted for username and password.

For each zone, you have the ability to determine the settings within each site (unless the IT department has locked down the desktop so no changes can be made to IE). Clicking the Custom Level button brings up the Security Settings dialog box, as shown in Figure 2.3. If you scroll down to the bottom of the list, you'll see the User Authentication section, with several options available under the Logon heading. If **Prompt for username and password** is checked, every time a SharePoint site is accessed, the user will have to enter his or her username and password, which gets very annoying. Changing this to **Automatic logon with current username and password** typically avoids this problem.

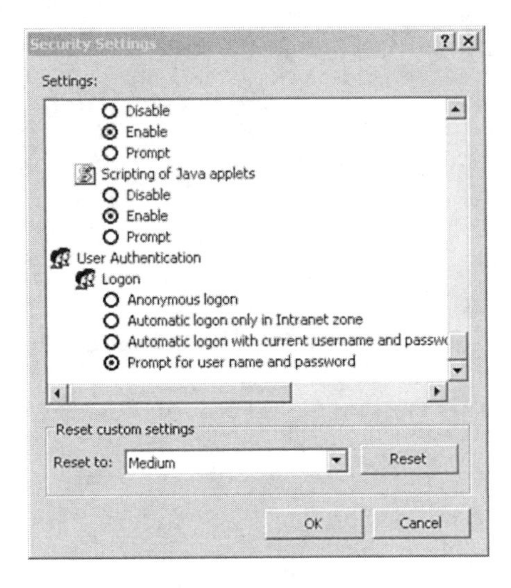

FIGURE 2.3 Security Settings dialog box.

Accessing the Advanced tab in the Internet Options dialog box provides access to many other custom configuration choices for IE, including Accessibility, Browsing, HTTP 1.1 settings, Microsoft VM, Multimedia, Printing, Search from the Address bar, and Security. In general, it is a good idea to stay away from the Advanced settings for IE 6.0 unless you have help desk support.

Using My Network Places

Another tool that's useful for the SharePoint user to become familiar with is My Network Places. This is quite simple to use and makes it very easy to save files to a favorite SharePoint site from within a standard application, because My Network Places will be presented as an option. For more adventurous users, navigating within My Network Places provides a unique view of the files that SharePoint contains and manages.

Assuming that you have Windows XP, to add a new network place, follow these steps:

1. Double-click the **My Network Places** icon.
2. Select the **Add a network place** icon.
3. When the Add Network Place Wizard opens, click **Next**.
4. Select **Choose another network connection** and then click **Next**.
5. Type in a URL (such as http://sp/sites/sitename) or click the **Browse** button to locate the SharePoint site you want to connect to. Click the **View some examples** hyperlink to see acceptable formats if needed. Click **Next**.
6. Type in a name for the new network place. Try to make the name as specific as possible because it can be difficult to find the right network place if your list gets lengthy. Click **Next**.
7. The final screen of the wizard will ask you to confirm your work. If you want to now open the network place, leave the box checked next to **Open this network place when I click Finish**. Click **Finish**.

At this point you will see a display similar to the one in Figure 2.4, which shows the contents of the site (in this case, ProServices). Because this site is a template and hasn't had any additional lists or libraries created in it, the structure is fairly simple and contains the _private, images, Lists, and Shared Documents folders. You can double-click any of these folders to see the contents. Depending on your rights within the document library folder, you can add or delete documents at this point, or you can create a new folder.

A common question that many new users ask is, Where do these files live? The documents and data files are actually stored by the SQL 2000 database (or the MSDE database, which is SQL 2000 "lite"), so you won't be able to find the actual files by browsing directories on the server that houses SharePoint.

FIGURE 2.4 View of a SharePoint network place.

CAUTION Be careful not to delete files in a SharePoint folder if you have Administrative rights on the site because this can damage the site and stop it from functioning properly.

Summary

This lesson covered two important tools for accessing SharePoint sites: Internet Explorer 6.0 and My Network Places. IE is easy to use on the surface, but it hides a large number of configuration options "under the hood." This lesson also gives some insight into using favorites, IE zones, and working with the user authentication settings.

The process of adding a network place is described, along with using the network place to see the folders and files with a SharePoint site.

LESSON 3
SharePoint Site Collections Demystified

In this lesson you will learn about site collections and their main components—top-level sites and subsites—and about document and meeting workspaces.

Site Collections, Top-level Sites, and Subsites Defined

Although the average SharePoint user may not have the rights to create site collections, subsites, document workspaces, or meeting workspaces, it is important to understand what each of these items is, because they are confusing to many new users. This information will also aid you in understanding the overall structure of the SharePoint environment and in building on the skills covered in Lesson 2, "Accessing SharePoint Sites," when navigating a SharePoint environment.

Figure 3.1 provides examples of Windows SharePoint Services and SharePoint Portal Server 2003 site collections. A site collection consists of a top-level site, subsites, and the content contained in those sites. Document workspaces and meeting workspaces can also be contained within site collections, and they are essentially sites themselves but are designed for specific purposes that will be discussed in this lesson.

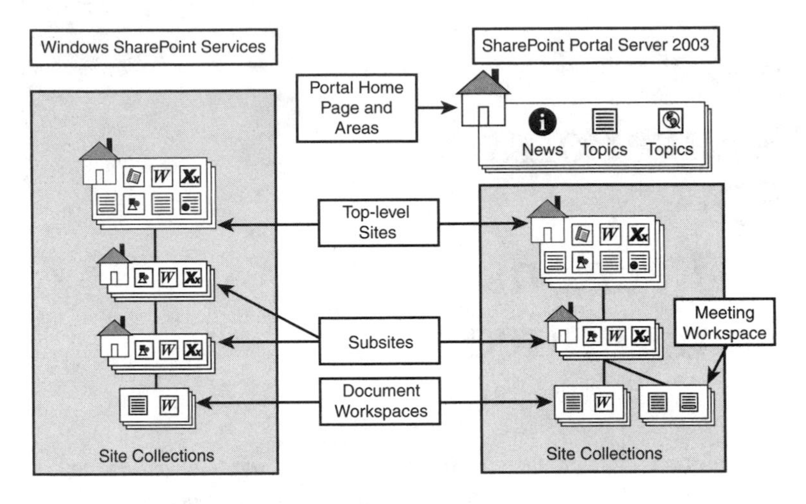

FIGURE 3.1 Diagram of site collections.

Note that site collections exist in both Windows SharePoint Services and SharePoint Portal Server 2003. Windows SharePoint Services is essentially a number of site collections, whereas SharePoint Portal Server 2003 provides a portal environment at the top and site collections beneath it. When a site is created in Windows SharePoint Services and it is not being created below another site, it is called a *top-level site*. When SharePoint Portal Server 2003 is in place, a site created beneath the portal is a top-level site. A top-level site can have subsites, and those subsites can have subsites, and so on. A top-level site or subsite can also have workspaces created underneath it.

Lesson 23, "Creating Sites," provides more information on creating sites for Site Administrators because the average user will not have the necessary rights to create top-level sites and subsites.

Site Groups

This is a good time to cover the very important topic of site groups because it is important for Site Administrators to control who has access to their site collections. A Site Administrator can specify who can perform which actions in the site by adding users to SharePoint site groups. Larger organizations may already have Active Directory groups created that can be added to site groups, which can be a great timesaver.

Here's a list of the standard site groups:

- **Reader**—Has read-only access to the site.
- **Contributor**—Can add content to existing document libraries and lists.
- **Web Designer**—Can create lists and document libraries and customize pages in the website.
- **Administrator**—Has full control of the website.
- **Custom Site Group**—A Site Administrator can actually create a site group and call it whatever he or she wants (Super Reader, Limited Contributor, Power User, and so on).

A Site Administrator can grant special access to Web Parts within the site (such as a document library), so if you really need to be able to add documents to a document library, but are only a member of the Reader site group, the Site Administrator can give you enhanced rights to that library.

CAUTION The assumption in Parts I–IV is that you are a member of the Contributor site group. If you are a member of the Reader site group, you won't have access to all the tools discussed in the end-user lessons. So it's a good idea to ask your Site Administrator which group or groups you are a member of if you don't already know.

Subsites Defined

Subsites can be created beneath top-level sites. They can contain the same elements that top-level sites can contain (document libraries, lists, Web Parts, and so on) but typically are designed to provide information to a subset of the users of the top-level site that is related to the top-level site's functionality. For example, a top-level site might be created for a department, such as Engineering, and subsites created below it for divisions of the department, such as Electrical Engineering and Mechanical Engineering. Alternatively, a top-level site might be created for the Sales department, and subsites created for key clients or projects.

It is important for the organization to think through the design of the Windows SharePoint Services site collections and SharePoint Portal Server 2003 environment to ensure that the right top-level sites and subsites are created for the user community. There needs to be a good combination of features and functionality so that top-level sites are available for the appropriate departments, committees, or groups and that the appropriate subsites are created, while ensuring that the SharePoint environment is navigable and manageable.

The structure of site collections is important for several additional reasons. The administrator of the top-level site can control settings for the top-level site and any subsites beneath it. Also, if the top-level site is moved or deleted, the subsites will be too. The subsites can also inherit rights from the top-level site, use the site groups available in the top-level site, and access Web Parts stored in the top-level site. The administrator of a subsite, however, can control settings for only that subsite, and the administrator of the next subsite can control settings only for that subsite.

Creating a Subsite

If an administrator or user with the right to create sites and subsites clicks the **Create** link in the top navigation bar of the site home page, he or she will see a fairly long list of options, which includes Document Libraries, Picture Libraries, Lists, Custom Lists, Discussion Boards, Surveys and ends with Web pages.

If **Sites and Workspaces** is clicked, the user or administrator will then need to enter some information about the site, such as its title, description, URL name, and whether it will use the permissions of the parent site or have unique permissions. Then a site template can be chosen from a list, as shown in Figure 3.2.

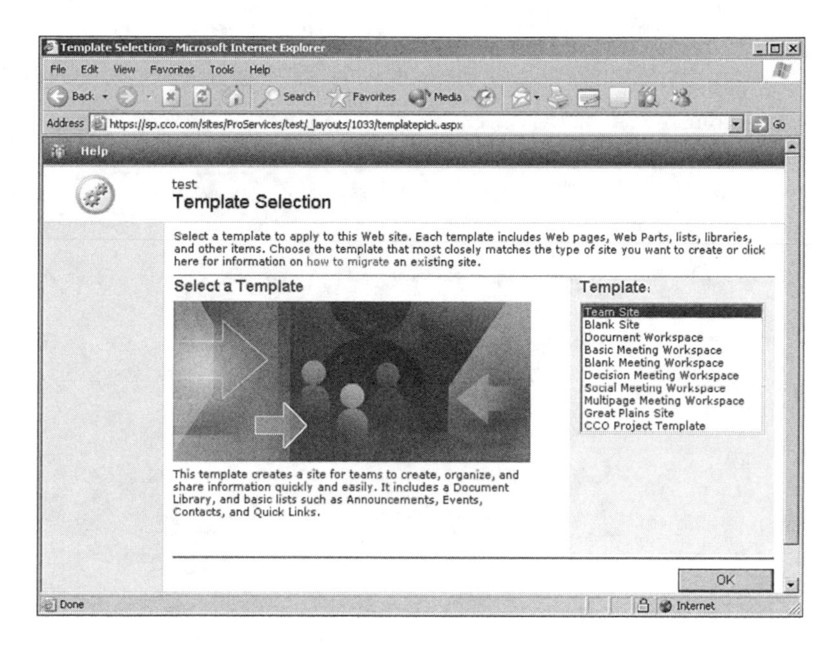

FIGURE 3.2 Template selection for the new site or workspace.

In this example the template list contains standard choices, including Team Site, Blank Site, Document Workspace, several Meeting Workspace choices, Great Plains Site, and CCO Project Template. All these are standard choices with the exception of the CCO Project Template, which was created by the Site Administrator and saved to the portal so that it would be available to all top-level sites and subsites. The Great Plains Site template is also not a standard template. Lesson 23, "Creating Sites," provides additional information about the different site templates.

Workspaces Defined

A workspace is essentially just another subsite that is created by a user or administrator with the Create Subsites right using a workspace template. If the Document Workspace option was selected in Figure 3.2, the results would appear as shown in Figure 3.3.

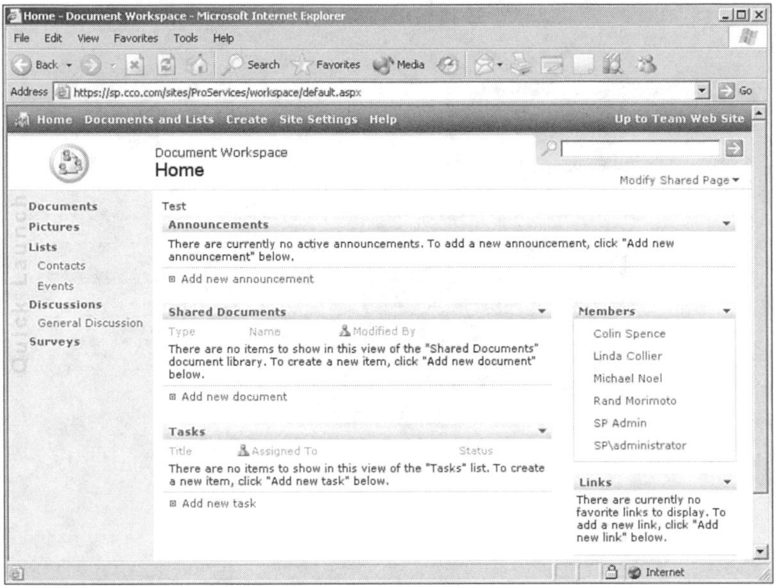

FIGURE 3.3 Document Workspace home page.

The workspace site includes the navigation bar at the top of the screen, the Quick Launch bar on the left, and a number of Web Parts, including Announcements, Shared Documents, Tasks, Members, and Links. The Members Web Part shows the users who have access to the workspace, which in this example include five domain accounts and a sixth account that's a local administrator account on the SharePoint server. Note that in the address bar, the new site is located under the ProServices site: .../sites/ProServices/workspace/default.aspx.

A document workspace can be created for collaboration among a select group of users, and the document would be stored in the document library. This is an alternative to the "old way" of sharing documents, where the document is emailed to a group of people who contribute to it, read it, or edit it and then send it back to a central point of contact. As most readers will attest, the email collaboration route works, but it can get confusing when the members of the team start making modifications, such as changing the title of the document, adding initials, and adding revision numbers. The central point of contact often needs to cut and paste between the different versions of the document or use Word's Compare and Merge Documents feature. With SharePoint there can be one copy of the document stored in a workspace, and only the team members can access it. As you will see in Lesson 5, "Document Library Basics," the tools provided in the document library make collaborating on a document extremely easy and versatile.

Meeting Workspaces

Figure 3.4 shows a sample meeting workspace that was created using the Basic Meeting Workspace template (refer to Figure 3.2) and updated with some sample content. This site contains an Objectives Web Part, along with Attendees, Agenda, and Document Library Web Parts. The intention of this site is to provide information that the meeting attendees need to have access to in advance of the meeting, as well as to define the agenda of the meeting.

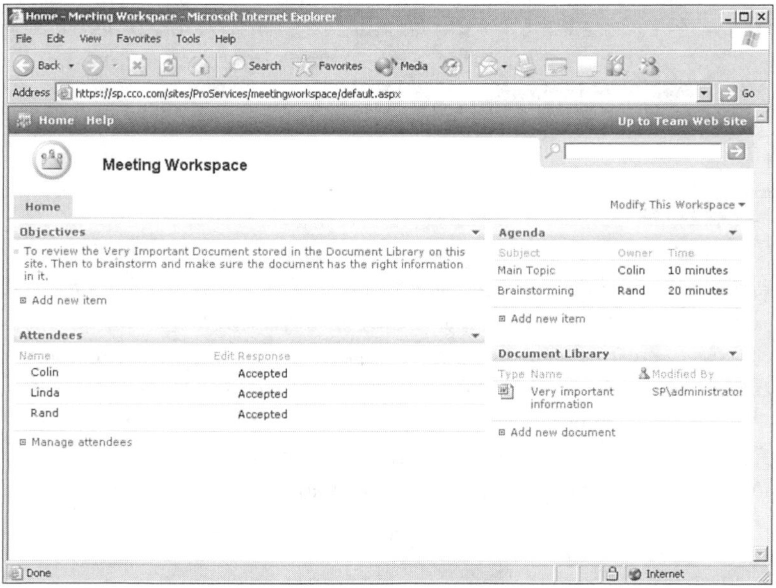

FIGURE 3.4 Meeting Workspace home page.

The creator of the workspace now has the ability to customize the workspace by adding additional Web Parts or content. You can imagine that a workspace created for a company trip or larger event could become quite complicated, but this is an excellent way to provide a centralized source of information for all attendees. As you'll see in Lesson 12, "Alerts and Document Versioning," alerts can be set by site members so they are sent an email if content in specified Web Parts change.

> **TIP** Be aware that workspaces can also be created from outside of SharePoint. For example, when a document is attached to an email in Outlook 2003, the user has the option of creating a document workspace to house the document and use that for collaborative purposes. Similarly, when a meeting is created in Outlook 2003, the option exists to create a meeting workspace, and the users invited to the meeting in Outlook will be able to access the site. Word 2003 and Excel 2003 offer similar features, where a document can be imbedded in a document workspace from these applications.

Summary

This lesson defined site collections, top-level sites, subsites, and document and meeting workspaces. The topic of site groups was covered briefly, and some insight into the significance of the top-level site was given. The process of creating a subsite or a workspace was introduced, even though the average user of a SharePoint site may not have the right to create one. The concept is important to understand, however, to become more comfortable with how SharePoint site collections are designed, and it introduces the templates that can be used for creating these subsites and workspaces.

LESSON 4
Introduction to Web Parts

In this lesson we'll look more closely at what Web Parts are, what they can do, and how to access the information in Web Parts.

What Is a Web Part?

Without getting too technical, a Web Part is a modular unit of information that has a specific purpose and that forms the basic building block of a SharePoint page. Web Parts are stored in a gallery (essentially a folder), which is in turn stored by the site or site collection, and can be added to the home page by Site Administrators.

Web Parts can technically perform just about any action possible on a website because they can contain programming code as well as provide access to data. The most commonly used Web Parts in SharePoint manage and provide access to data stored in the database. The data can be in the form of documents that are posted to libraries or in the form of data that is stored in tabular form and posted to lists.

> **NOTE** Let's clarify the difference between document libraries and lists: Document libraries contain documents (of any type that is allowed to be uploaded to a SharePoint library) and lists contain tabular information organized in columns and rows, similar to an Excel spreadsheet. Document libraries can have additional rows of information, called *metadata*, added by administrators.

Clicking the **Documents and Lists** link in the navigation bar on the home page will open a page that shows all the different lists and libraries contained within the site. Figure 4.1 shows the first five items for the sample ProServices site.

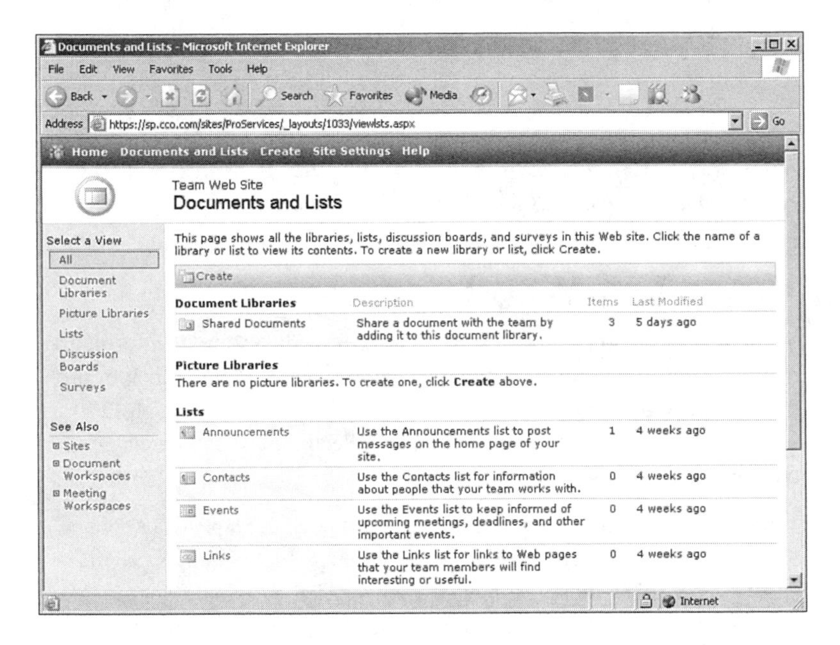

FIGURE 4.1 Documents and Lists viewing page.

This is a very quick way to see all the different libraries and lists stored in the site, all of which are Web Parts. Bear in mind that not all these may be shown on the home page of the site, or in the Quick Launch bar on the home page, because the Site Administrator decides which items to include for general viewing. Also, note that the See Also area on the left side of the screen in Figure 4.1 provides access to Sites, Document Workspaces, and Meetings Workspaces for a quick way to see which, if any, of those sites have been created.

Clicking the name of a document library or list will also open that library or list. So remembering the **Documents and Lists** link in the navigation bar is a quick-and-easy way to see the contents of the site.

Basic Web Part Components

In Lesson 1, "Introduction to SharePoint 2003," we looked at the main components of a SharePoint site, and a brief description was given of the different items you will see in a default team site. It was pointed out that a number of the items on the screen were actually Web Parts (Announcements, Events, Links, and the Windows SharePoint Services image).

In Figure 4.2 we see the same ProServices department team website shown previously.

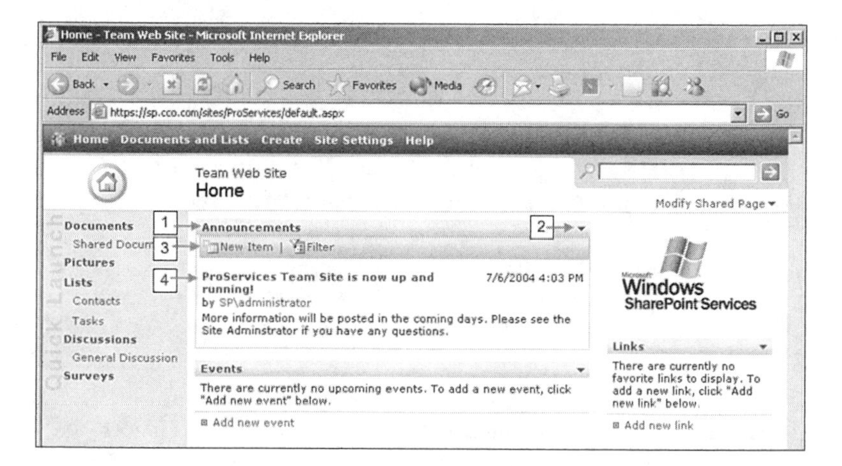

FIGURE 4.2 Web Part components.

From a functional standpoint, the Web Parts as they appear on the home page have several components, which are labeled in the figure for the Announcements Web Part:

1. **Title bar**—The title bar can be shown or hidden by a Site Administrator. The title itself can also be changed by a site administrator. Clicking the name of the Web Part in the title bar will open the Web Part to full-screen mode, as shown in Figure 4.3.

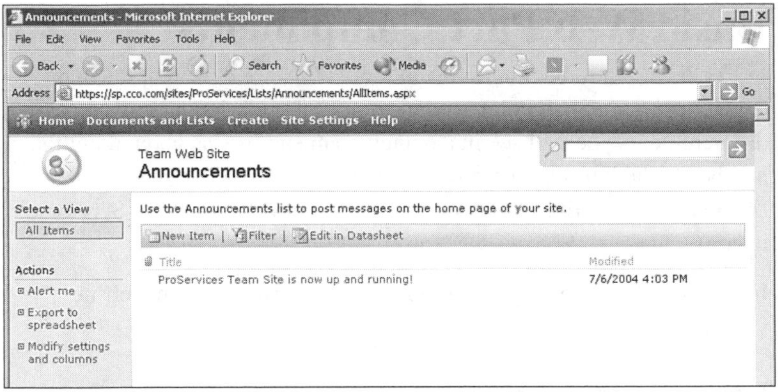

FIGURE 4.3 All Items view of a Web Part.

> **NOTE** Windows SharePoint Services uses ASP.NET Active Server Pages (or ASPX pages) for lists and forms. In Figure 4.3, note that the URL in the address bar is https://sp.cco.com/sites/ProServices/Lists/Announcements/AllItems.aspx. Therefore, the page that is displayed is the AllItems.aspx page.

2. **The down arrow in the title bar**—When clicked, this innocuous-looking arrow reveals additional functionality available for modifying the Web Part: Minimize, Close, Modify Shared Web Part, and Help. If you only have Reader rights on the site, you will only see the Help option. If you click Minimize, the contents of the Web Part will be hidden and all you will see is the title bar. If you click Close, the Web Part is removed from your view of the site.

> **TIP** Clicking the down arrow in the Web Part header and then clicking Help is a great way to find out more about Web Parts and accessing additional SharePoint help resources.

3. **The toolbar**—The toolbar provides tools that can be accessed from the home page that affect the contents of the Web Part, such as New Item and Filter. The toolbar can be hidden by a Site Administrator.

4. **Content**—Content can be in the form of text, such as in Figure 4.2 for the Announcement Web Part. If the Web Part is a document library, the document titles are shown, or if it is a Contacts Web Part, the contact names are shown. You can click the title of the announcement and the item will open up to full-screen view, as shown in Figure 4.4.

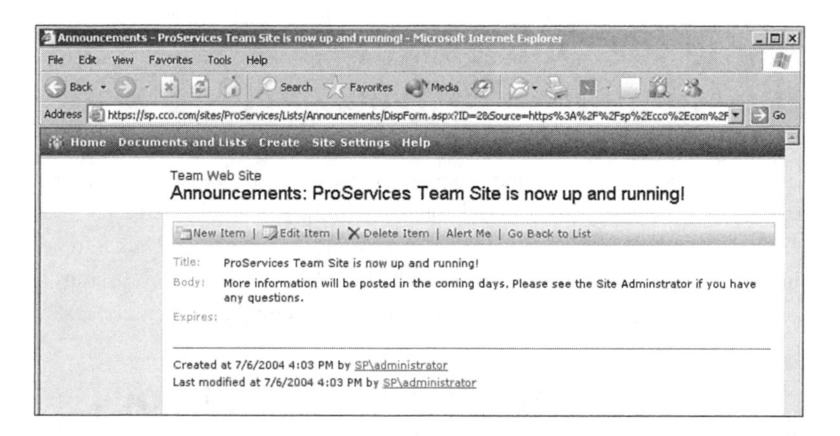

FIGURE 4.4 Announcements list display form.

A number of tools are available once you are viewing the item in the display form (in this case, New Item, Edit Item, Delete Item, Alert Me, and Go Back to List). These tools will be covered in depth in Parts II and III of this book. Once again, you need to have appropriate rights within the list to be able to add, edit, or delete items.

CAUTION The tools shown in Figure 4.4 will be the same even if you only have Reader rights to the list. You can even click the Delete Item tool and it will ask you to confirm that you do in fact want to delete the item. However, you will then be prompted for your username and password. After three failed attempts to request permission from SharePoint to perform the forbidden action, you will see a Request Access screen. This screen tells you that access is denied and you do not have permission to perform this action or access this resource. You can request that a Site Administrator give you elevated rights in the list by completing the form and then clicking the Send Request button.

Using the Quick Launch Bar to See the Contents of a Web Part

The Quick Launch bar on the left-hand side of the home page provides a quick way to get to the AllItems.aspx page, which displays the contents of the list or library. If you see the name of the library or list in the Quick Launch bar, click it to open the Web Part. Alternately, you can click a topic in the Quick Launch bar (such as Documents, Pictures, Lists, Discussions, or Surveys) and the viewlists.aspx page for that grouping will appear.

Two Different Views of the Home Page

There are two different views of the home page: the Shared View and the Personal View. Figure 4.5 shows the two options available when you click the **Modify Shared Page** drop-down menu. By default, the Shared View will be displayed when you visit the site, but by selecting the Personal View option (if you have rights to do so), you will see a personalized view.

Therefore, users with sufficient rights can actually customize the way the Web Parts on the page are displayed to suit their needs! A general recommendation is to use this power sparingly because the Site Administrators probably have put significant time and energy into the way the site looks and how information is displayed, and you may find yourself missing out on important information if you make too many changes. For example, if you close the Announcements Web Part for your Personal View, you may miss some important information.

> **NOTE** As well as being able to choose between the Personal and Shared views on the home page, you can choose different views from within the Web Part itself. The topic of the different views available within the Web Part is covered more in Lesson 11, "Modifying and Creating Views in Libraries and Lists."

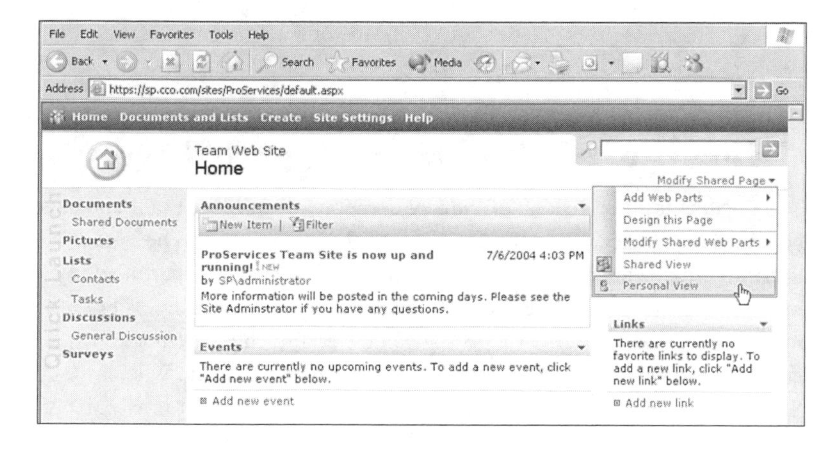

FIGURE 4.5 Shared View and Personal View options.

Summary

This lesson discussed what Web Parts are and how they are used in SharePoint. The main components of a typical Web Part (such as Announcements) were described as they appear on the home page, and different ways to access the contents of Web Parts were detailed (such as clicking **Documents and Lists** in the navigation bar and clicking the title of the Web Part). A high-level overview of what you can do within a Web Part was given, and this topic will also be covered in following lessons. Lastly, the two different views (Shared and Personal) of Web Parts on the site home page were introduced.

Lesson 5
Document Library Basics

In this lesson we will cover the basic features of a document library, one of the key Web Parts offered by SharePoint.

Overview of the Document Library

The document library is one of the key components of SharePoint and can be added to a site by using the Document Library Web Part. The organization can use document libraries to organize documents by department, by project, or by topic, and the Site Administrator can control the level of interaction different users of a library can have. Typically, the network administrators determine the rights to folders on the network, whereas SharePoint brings this level of control to the Site Administrator, who is often a department manager. So with SharePoint, a Site Administrator, who probably has no control over network-level file access, can fine-tune who can add, edit, and read the documents in a document library.

Once the files are stored within the document library, a number of customizations can be performed to enhance the functionality of the library and add value to the users. These are talked about throughout the book, but some examples include the following:

- **Metadata—**New columns can be added to the library that contain a variety of different textual or numeric information to better define the contents of the document, to help users find what they need more quickly. For example, a metadata column called Document Status could be added, with the values Draft, In Review, and Final, so anyone using the library can immediately tell the status of the document. Likewise, a metadata column called Page Count could be added that contains the length of the document. Lesson 9, "Introduction to Metadata," covers this topic in more depth.

- **Alerts**—A user can set an alert on a library or on a document itself. The alert process sends an email to the user when a certain event happens—such as an item is added to the library, an item is changed or deleted, or a Web discussion is added—and the alert can be sent out immediately, at the end of the day, or at the end of the week. This topic is covered in Lesson 12, "Alerts and Document Versioning."
- **Views**—The All Documents view can be fine-tuned to change how information is displayed, which columns of information are shown, and how the information is grouped. Also, total information can be provided on numerical information contained in columns. Filters can be applied so that only documents that meet certain criteria are displayed (for example, only documents that are in final status will appear). Lesson 11, "Modifying and Creating Views in Libraries and Lists," covers views in more depth.

Figure 5.1 shows a sample document library that contains one document, titled "Document A." A document library can be accessed from the home page by clicking the title of the library in the Quick Launch bar or by clicking the title of the document library if it appears on the home page. A slightly more complex way to access the document library is to click **Documents and Lists** from the home page and then click the appropriate document library name in the Document Libraries section.

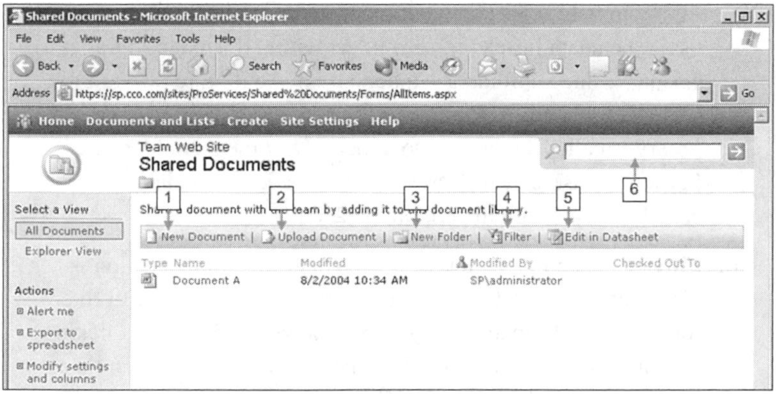

FIGURE 5.1 Sample document library.

1. **New Document**—By clicking the New Document button, the user can create a new document based on the template that has been assigned to the document library. This could be a blank Word document, a FrontPage Web page, an Excel spreadsheet, a PowerPoint presentation, a Basic Page, or a Web Part page—or there could be no template assigned. If no template is assigned, a blank Word document will open when the user clicks New Document.

> **TIP** The proper use of templates can be a great way to save time when many similar documents are being created. For example, a Site Administrator might use a customized Word document for a template in the Sales Document document library that has the company logo on it, appropriate header and footer information, and perhaps an outline of the approved format for the document.

2. **Upload Document**—This tool allows a user with Insert Items permission to upload documents to the library. This process is discussed in more detail in the following section in this lesson.

3. **New Folder**—Folders can be created within the document library to help organize the documents by subtopics. Consider using metadata instead of subfolders within document libraries because using subfolders can actually make it more difficult to find what you are looking for. For example, if the document library is called Technical Documents, and the subfolders are Phase 1, Phase 2, and Phase 3, why not add a metadata column called "Phase" with the options 1, 2, and 3?

4. **Filter**—When this button is clicked, additional information is displayed within the document library to allow the user to filter for specific information. Figure 5.2 shows the results of clicking the Filter button, where the file type options are shown and the user only wants to see the DOC file types. This can be extremely useful when a large number of documents is in the library and the user wants to find a specific subset.

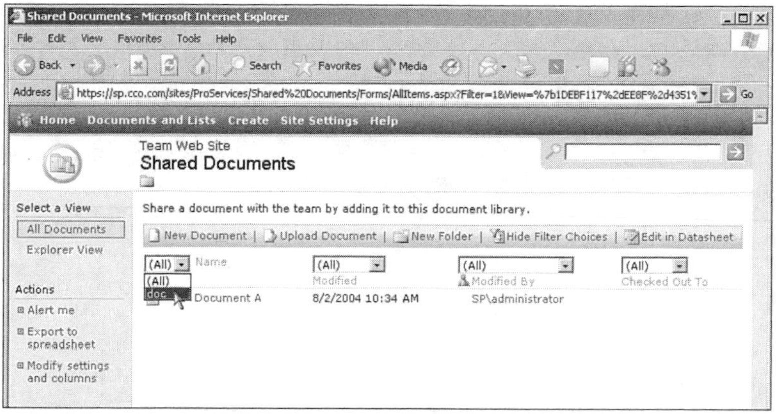

FIGURE 5.2 Filter options.

5. **Edit in Datasheet**—This tool will be discussed in more detail in Lesson 10, "The Datasheet and Explorer Views." For now, though, it's enough to know that the Datasheet view requires Excel 2003 be installed on the workstation of the user accessing the library to function. The Datasheet view is very helpful for accessing some advanced functionality of libraries and lists, for inputting information to metadata columns, and working with Excel and Access.

6. **Search bar**—If the user enters a word in the search bar from within a document library, SharePoint will search within the contents of the files within the library only, and the results will appear almost immediately.

How to Upload a Document

To upload a document, the user first needs to have the appropriate rights in the document library to do so. The process is as follows:

1. Click **Upload Document** from within the document library, and the interface shown in Figure 5.3 appears.

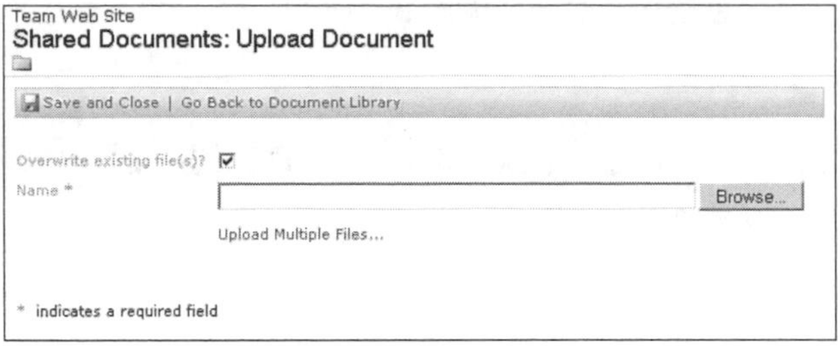

FIGURE 5.3 Upload Document page.

2. Click the **Browse** button, and the **Choose file** window opens, allowing you to browse the network or your local drives for the desired document.

3. Select the document to upload and click the **Open** button.

4. The name and path of the document should appear in the **Name** field. Click **Save and Close**. Note that if the library has metadata columns added, some additional fields may need to be filled out at this point. If a field has a red asterisk next to it, you must fill it out before the document can be uploaded. Although this might require a few extra minutes of work, it adds value to the document library by helping users find the document that best meets their needs.

5. The document will be uploaded to the library (unless it is of a file type that is not permitted, thus generating an error message). If the **Overwrite existing file(s)?** box is checked, the new document will overwrite a document of the same name in the document library. The new document will typically be tagged with "!New" in green text, which remains for 24 hours.

If Office 2003 is installed on your computer, you will see the Upload Multiple Files option. Clicking this option will bring up a more complex interface, as shown in Figure 5.4. From this interface, you can choose multiple documents in the same directory and then click the **Save and Close** button. Note that you can't select a file from one directory and then select a file from a different directory. Only the files selected on the screen will be saved when Save and Close is clicked.

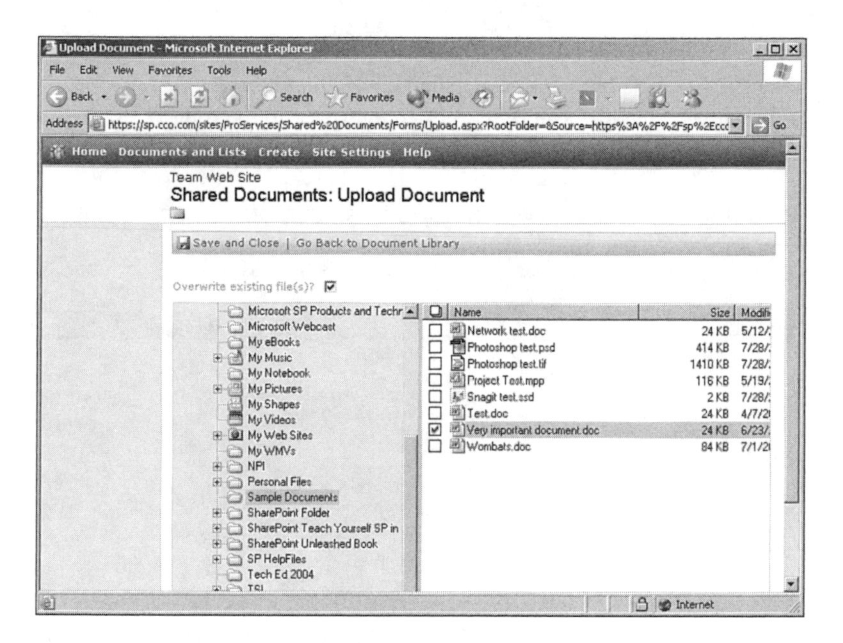

FIGURE 5.4 Upload Multiple Documents page.

> **TIP** You can also use the Explorer view to upload documents, and this will be covered in Lesson 10. This is often the recommended way to move a large number of files to a SharePoint document library.

Working with Documents in the Library

Now that there are documents in the document library, a number of activities can take place. One of the most common is for users to edit these documents. If a user only has Read privileges in the document library, she won't be able to edit the document and save it back to the library. The user needs Edit permissions to modify a document and save it back to the library.

Figure 5.5 shows the commands available when a user hovers the mouse over the filename of the document and clicks the black down arrow. Alternatively, the user can right-click in the space to the right of the filename (this can sometimes be easier than clicking the black arrow).

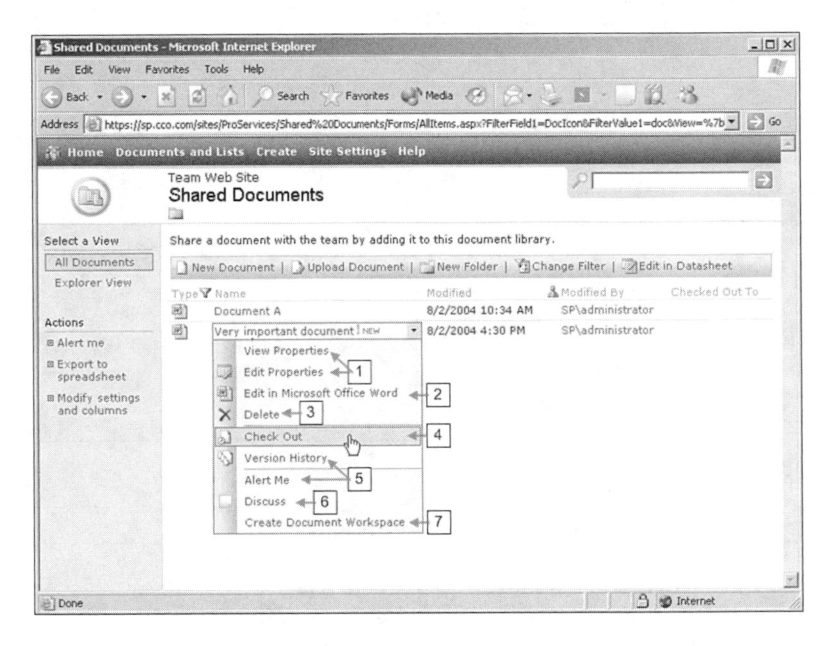

FIGURE 5.5 Document actions

1. **View Properties and Edit Properties**—These commands allow the user to view or edit the document properties. Not all document properties are editable because some information is generated automatically, such as Modified Time and Modified By, but the name of the document and the title of the document can be modified by someone with Edit privileges. If metadata columns appear in the library, they can be edited here or in Datasheet view.

2. **Edit in Microsoft Word**—This is the preferred method of editing a Microsoft document stored in a document library, and the command will reflect the application used to create the file (for example, an Excel file would have **Edit in Microsoft Excel** as the option in this menu).

3. **Delete**—A user needs Delete privileges to delete files within a document library. If versioning is on, all previous versions will be deleted.

> **CAUTION** There is no undelete function by default in SharePoint. When you delete a file from a document library, it cannot be restored by clicking **Undo**, and will not appear in your Recycle Bin on your desktop. Typically, you will need to approach a Site Administrator to recover an accidentally deleted file.

4. **Check Out**—A recommended best practice is to "check out" a document before you start working on it. This locks the file in SharePoint so no one else can save over it, and it lets other users of the library know that you have it reserved. You don't actually have to edit it at that exact moment. A Site Administrator can force a check-in if you forget to check it in yourself.

5. **Version History and Alert Me**—Version History provides access to a list of previous versions of the document, if versioning is activated for the document library. Alert Me sends an email alert if changes are made to the document. These commands will be discussed in Lesson 12.

6. **Discuss**—A Web Discussion allows a user to attach notes to items on the page. These won't be discussed in detail because they aren't typically used by most clients, and it is generally recommended that discussions take place in a SharePoint Discussion Group Web Part rather than in a Web Discussion. Feel free to experiment with this tool if you like.

7. **Create Document Workspace**—Document workspaces were discussed in Lesson 3, "SharePoint Site Collections Demystified." This command provides a handy way to create a workspace "around" a document that is stored in a document library. If you have rights to create a document workspace and click this command, you will see the message that appears in Figure 5.6. If you click **OK**, a workspace will be created that

contains a copy of the document (in this case, Very important document.doc) .

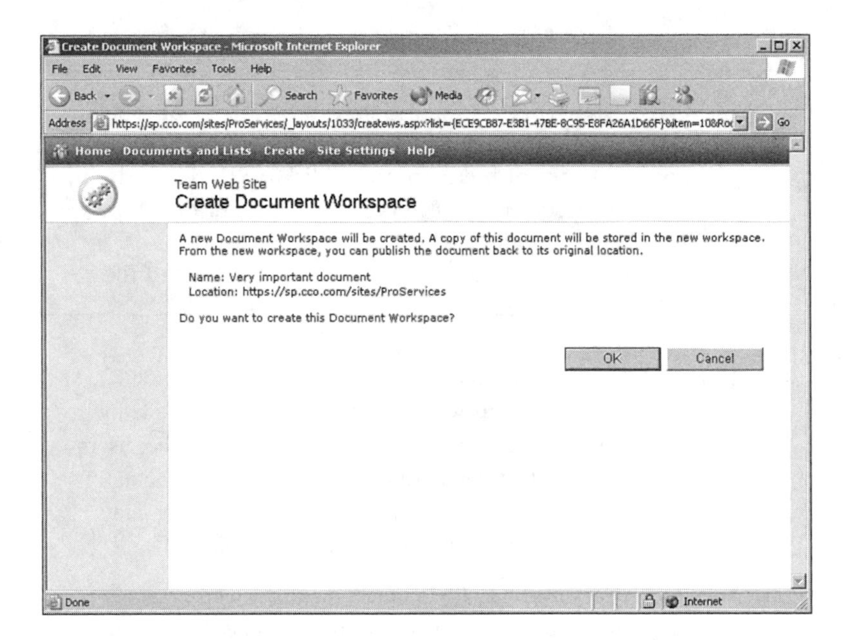

FIGURE 5.6 Create Document workspace with a document library.

Summary

This lesson covered the basics of a document library, preparing you for coverage of the more advanced features and tools that can be used in a library or list. The process of creating a new document from within a document library was covered, as well as uploading single documents and multiple documents, creating a new folder, filtering content, and searching for a word contained by a document in the library. The different actions that can be performed on a document were outlined, and some of these will be covered further in future lessons.

LESSON 6
Picture Library Basics

In this lesson we will look at the basic features of a picture library for an overview of how SharePoint handles the storage and management of images.

Basic Features of the Picture Library

A picture library is very similar to a document library in that it's also a Web Part designed to store documents and allow users to attach metadata to the documents. The picture library is designed with the assumption that users will want to store graphics files in the library. Thus, the Marketing department might create one picture library on its home page for approved logo files and another one for graphics and photographs for use in publications. Or, the Human Resources department might create a picture library for company events and then create subfolders for different events, such as the Christmas party and company picnic.

Creating a Picture Library

In the ProServices site we have been working with, a heading titled "Pictures" appears on the Quick Launch bar, but no libraries are listed under the heading, which means that no picture libraries have been created yet.

To create a picture library (if you have the appropriate rights), you can do one of two things: You can use the **Create** command, or you can click **Pictures** in the Quick Launch bar.

Creating a Picture Library with the Create Command

1. Click **Create** on the home page.
2. Click **Picture Library** (the third option from the top).
3. Provide the information requested in the New Picture Library page, as shown in Figure 6.1. Enter the name of the library, a description (which will appear in the AllItems.aspx view of the Web Part), choose whether you want the library to appear on the Quick Launch bar, and choose whether you want a new version of the graphics file to be created each time the file is edited.

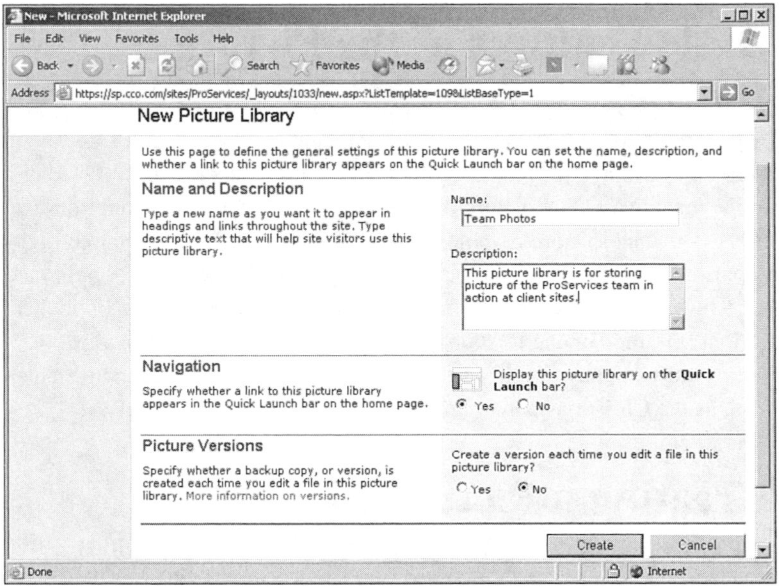

FIGURE 6.1 New Picture Library page.

4. Click **Create** and the picture library is created.

Creating a Picture Library by Clicking Pictures in the Quick Launch Bar

1. Click **Pictures** in the Quick Launch bar from the home page of the site.
2. Click **Create Picture Library** in the toolbar.
3. Click **Picture Library** under the heading Picture Libraries.
4. Enter the same information as listed in step 3 in the previous section.
5. Click **Create** and the picture library is created.

Using the Picture Library

The resulting library will be empty, and the uploading process is similar to what was covered for the document library in Lesson 5, "Document Library Basics." To upload a single document, simply click the **Add Picture** button in the toolbar in the Picture Library page (listed as AllItems.aspx in the URL address) and then browse for the file.

If you have Office 2003 installed and want to upload multiple files, the process is a little different because SharePoint will open the Microsoft Office Picture Manager program to allow you to choose multiple files.

NOTE If you don't have Office 2003 installed, you won't see the option to upload multiple files.

Figure 6.2 shows the interface when you click **Add Picture,** then choose the Upload Multiple Files option from the Add Picture page (the Upload.aspx page in the URL address).

Several things are worth covering briefly in the Picture Manager, as numbered in the figure:

1. To select multiple image files, you need to hold the **Ctrl** key and click each file. In this figure, the three images have been selected, as evidenced by the gray borders around the image previews.

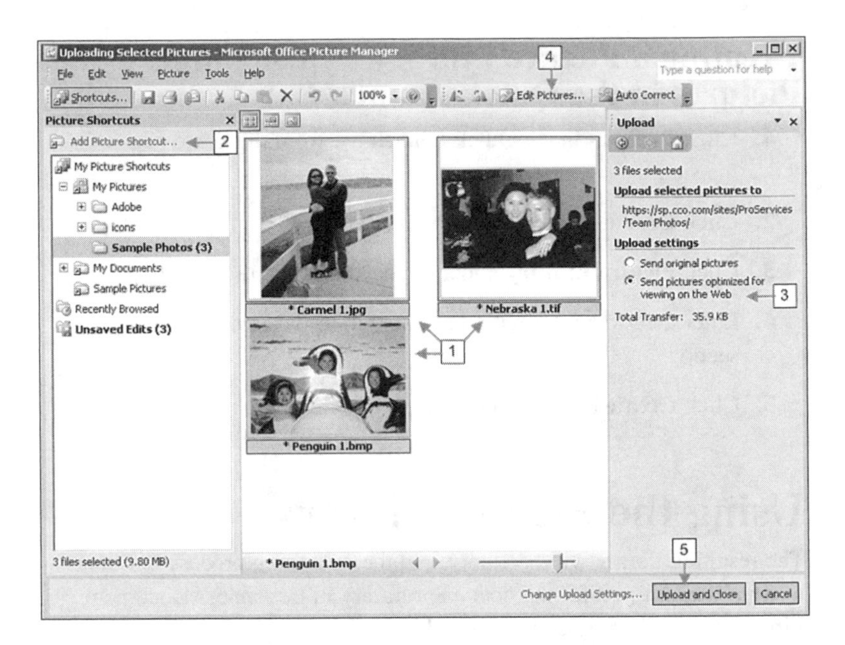

FIGURE 6.2 Upload multiple images using Microsoft Office Picture Manager.

2. If the folder doesn't show up in the Picture Shortcuts area, you may need to click **Add Picture Shortcuts** and find the directory that contains the image files.

3. Clicking the **Upload settings** option **Send picture optimized for viewing on the Web** can save a great deal of time, if the quality of the image isn't that critical. In the case of these three sample images, the total transfer size was 9.8MB originally, but it went down to 35.9KB when the optimized option was selected.

4. Some editing tools are made available when you click the Edit Pictures button in the toolbar. These include Brightness and Contrast, Color, Crop, Rotate and Flip, Red Eye Removal, Resize, and Compress Picture.

5. Finally, once you have the images selected, you can click **Upload and Close**.

Once the images have been uploaded, you may have to click **Go back to "Team Photos"** (or the name of your picture library). You'll then see something like what's shown Figure 6.3, with the images displayed in the Thumbnails view.

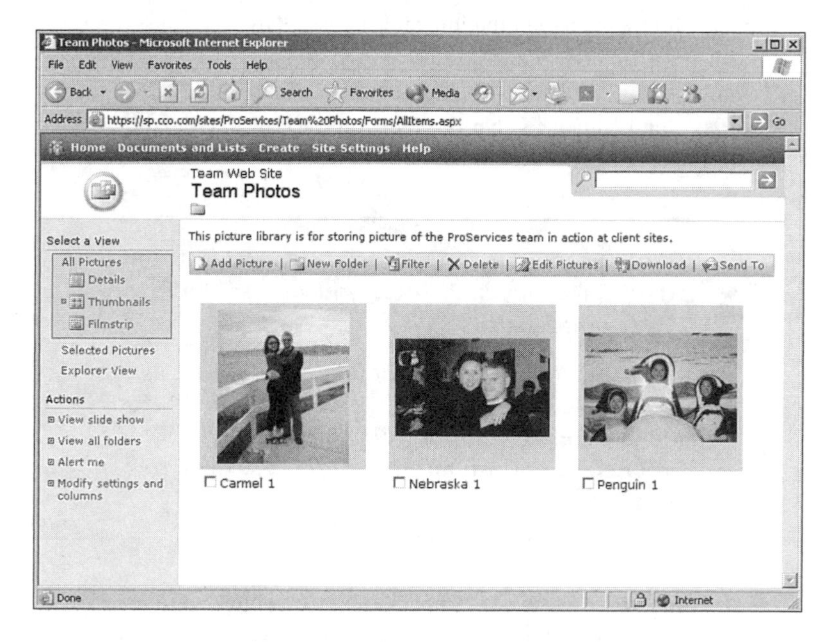

FIGURE 6.3 The picture library's All Items view.

Tools Available in the Picture Library

If you have read Lesson 5, several of the tools discussed here will be familiar to you. Add Picture is the equivalent of Upload Document, and New Folder allows you to create a folder within the library. The Filter feature was also covered in Lesson 5. A Delete button is also offered in the picture library toolbar, along with several others: Edit Pictures, Download, and Send To.

Note that each image in the Thumbnails view has a check box under it. Checking the box next to an image or several images allows you to use the Edit Pictures, Download, and Send To tools. These tools are detailed in the following list:

- **Edit Pictures**—When this button is clicked, the Microsoft Office Picture Manager (shown previously in Figure 6.2) opens and allows you to edit the image. Microsoft Office Picture Manager supports viewing, editing, and compressing the following file types: JPEG, TIFF, GIF, PNG, and BMP. WMF/EMF files aren't editable. Other file types aren't viewable or editable in Picture Manager.

> **CAUTION** If you don't have Office 2003 installed, when you click Edit Pictures, you will see the following error message:
>
> "This feature requires a Windows SharePoint Services-compatible control, such as Microsoft Office Picture Manager. Either the control is not installed or your browser is not configured to support ActiveX controls."

- **Download**—Any selected images can be downloaded to your local hard drive. When you click this button, you will see the Download Photos page, shown in Figure 6.4. This page enables you to select the size of the images (Full Size, 640×480, or 160×120), set advanced download options, and send pictures to another application. Although we don't have space to cover these options in detail, the advanced download options allow you to change the file format, set a custom width and height, and change the percentage size of the image(s) . If **Send picture to** is selected (and Office 2003 is installed), you have the option of sending the picture(s) to an Office document you currently have open, an Outlook message, a Word document, a PowerPoint presentation, or an Excel worksheet. This can be quite a timesaver!

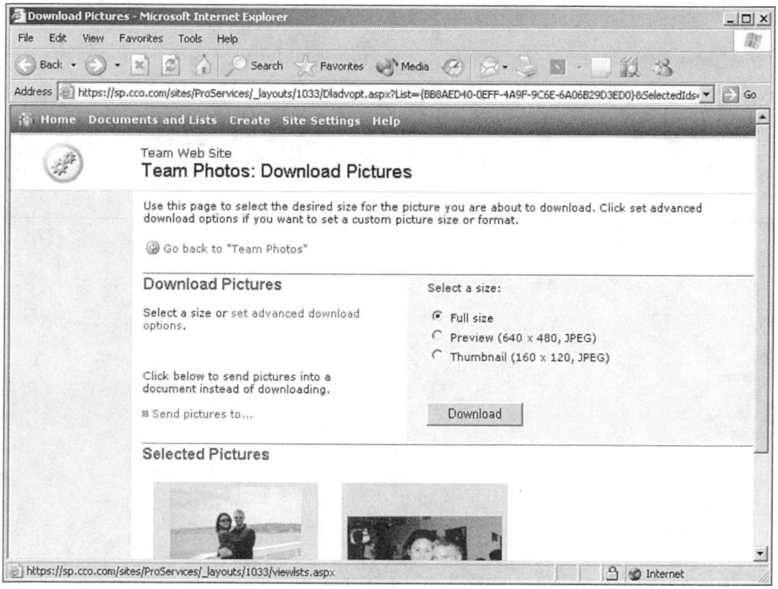

FIGURE 6.4 Download Pictures page.

- **Send To**—If you have Office 2003 installed, the Send To option allows you to send the image(s) selected to an Office document you currently have open, an Outlook message, a Word document, a PowerPoint presentation, or an Excel worksheet.

Accessing Additional Tools Within the Library

When you are in the Thumbnails view (which can be selected on the left side of the page) in the picture library, you won't have access to the drop-down menu discussed in Lesson 5, which is available when you hover the mouse over the filename and click the down arrow. As shown in Figure 6.5, to access the additional tools available in this menu, such as **Check Out** and **Version History**, you need to click the **Details view** (circled in Figure 6.5). Then the menu will be available when you hover the mouse over the filename and click on the down arrow.

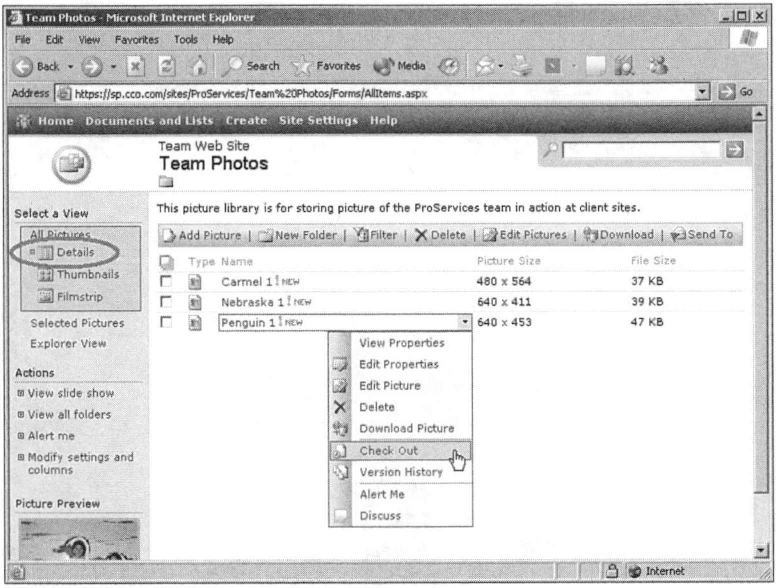

FIGURE 6.5 Additional tools available in Details view.

The tools offered in this menu are similar to those available in the document library, with the addition of the Download Picture option.

Picture Properties

When in the Details view of the picture library, if you select **Edit Properties**, you can edit the picture properties, as shown in Figure 6.6. This is where additional information, such as title, the date the picture was taken, and keywords, can be entered about the images uploaded to the picture library. This information is searchable in SharePoint, so it is helpful to add it to uploaded images. If metadata has been added to the library, it will also be available for editing.

If you click the preview image shown in the EditForm.aspx page (as shown in Figure 6.6), the image will be shown without property information, and the address bar will show the full picture name and location. In the case of this example, the picture filename and location is https://sp.cco.com/sites/ProServices/Team%20Photos/Carmel%201.jpg.

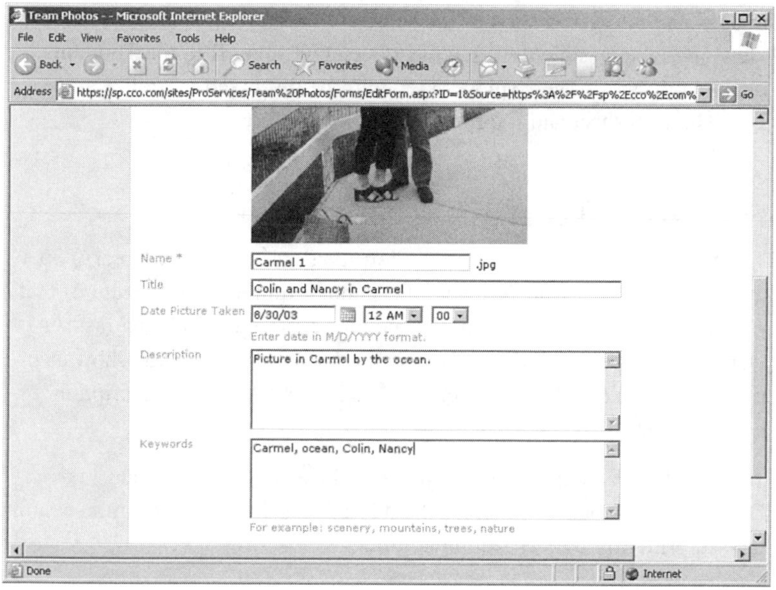

FIGURE 6.6 Edit properties of an image.

Note the "%20" in the filename. This is how HTML refers to a space in the filename, so don't be alarmed. This file location can now be used to send people directly to the file, so the whole file doesn't need to be forwarded. This can be very handy with large files, and it can cut down on the size of email attachments. Of course, the person trying to access the image via the URL will need to have access to the picture library.

Different Views Available

The menu bar on the left side of the picture library (the AllItems.aspx page as shown in Figure 6.3) offers several different view choices. So far you have seen examples of the Thumbnails view, which is very helpful if you want to see what the image looks like at reduced resolution, and the Details view, which provides access to additional tools via the drop-down menu.

The Filmstrip view is also offered, as well as the Selected Pictures view and the Explorer view. The Filmstrip view shows the smaller preview images and a larger version of the selected image. The Selected Pictures view only displays pictures that have been checked off in the Thumbnails or Filmstrip view. The Explorer View will be discussed more in Lesson 10, "The Datasheet and Explorer Views."

Actions Menu

The **View slide show** action (on the left menu of the picture library) opens up a slide show window (Office 2003 is not required for this feature) that provides standard VCR buttons—play, pause, stop, rewind, and fast forward—to present the different images in the library. The slide show also provides the name of the image, the date it was taken, and description information.

The **Alert me** action will be discussed in Lesson 12, "Alerts and Document Versioning," whereas the **Modify settings and columns** action is used primarily by Site Administrators.

Summary

This lesson covered the basic features of the picture library, including the steps required to create a picture library. The process of uploading multiple image files is covered because it is different from uploading multiple files to a document library. The Edit Picture, Download and Send To tools were also covered. The different views available in the picture library were covered briefly, along with the slide show feature. After completing this lesson, you should have a better understanding of the features of the picture library and have some idea of how it can be used in your organization.

LESSON 7

Using the Links, Contacts, and Events Lists

In this lesson we will look at the links, contacts, and events lists that are standard Web Parts used in many standard SharePoint websites.

The Links List

The links list is present on many SharePoint sites and is included in several of the standard templates, including the Team Site template and the Document Workspace template. This Web Part is pretty self-explanatory and doesn't include very many special features. The main use is to provide easy access to websites that would be of particular interest to a user of the site. These can be sites on the same SharePoint server, such as other departments, or external sites, perhaps those of business partners, or even reference sites containing technical reference materials.

Figure 7.1 shows a sample links list with three entries in it. This list can be accessed by clicking the title of the links list from the site home page, by clicking the name of the links list from the Quick Launch bar on the left side of the home page, or by clicking **Documents and Lists** in the navigation bar on the home page and then selecting the links list.

To add a new link, you simply click **New Item** in the menu bar, as shown in Figure 7.1. Once the New Item page (referenced as the NewForm.aspx page in the URL) is open, simply enter in the following information:

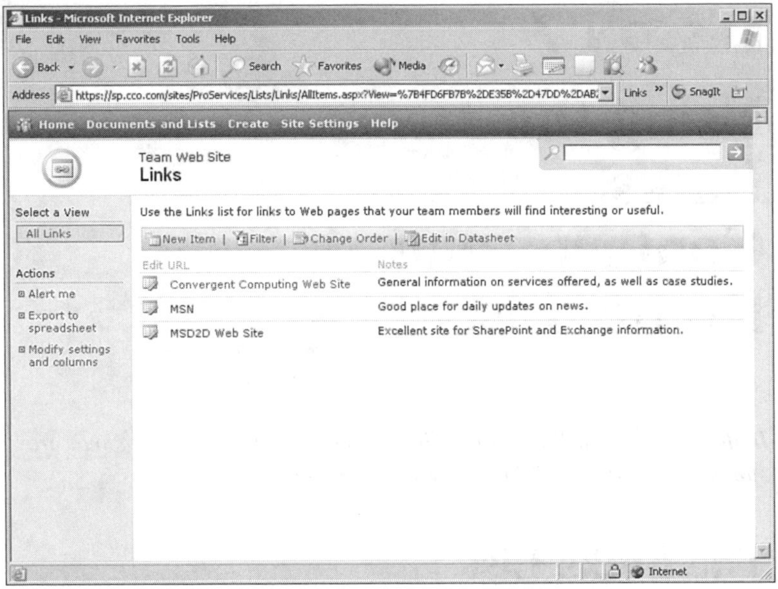

FIGURE 7.1 List Web Part AllItems page.

- **The URL**—You can type it in from memory if it's short, or open another instance of IE, go to the site, select and copy the entire URL (**Ctrl+C**), and then paste (**Ctrl+V**) it back in the NewForm.aspx page. Once the URL has been entered, you can click **Click here** to test above the field to make sure you entered it properly and to make sure SharePoint can actually talk to the server housing the URL.
- **A description**—This is what shows up on the home page, and it is recommended that you make it short and descriptive.
- **Notes**—Notes are optional, and they are viewable from the AllItems.aspx page.

Another useful tool in the links list view (referenced as AllItems.aspx in the URL) is the **Change Order** tool, which, as the name implies, let's you assign a number to each entry that corresponds to its position from the top of the list. If you have sufficient rights, this allows you, or the Site Administrator, to determine the exact order in which these items are arranged.

> **TIP** Note that you can add a link to a specific document or a specific document library on a SharePoint site if you have the whole URL.

The Contacts List

The contacts list is also a standard component of many websites that can be used to provide a central "yellow pages" of contacts for the users of the site. For example, in the ProServices site we have been working on, the contacts list could contain a list of all the members of the ProServices department, their cell phone numbers, email addresses, and other information.

Figure 7.2 provides a view of a sample contacts list with four entries. The contacts list (referenced as AllItems.apsx in the URL) provides the New Item, Filter, Edit in Datasheet, Link to Outlook, and Import Contacts tools. The All Contacts view is offered by default. In this example, all the contacts have been newly added, so are tagged with the "!new" label.

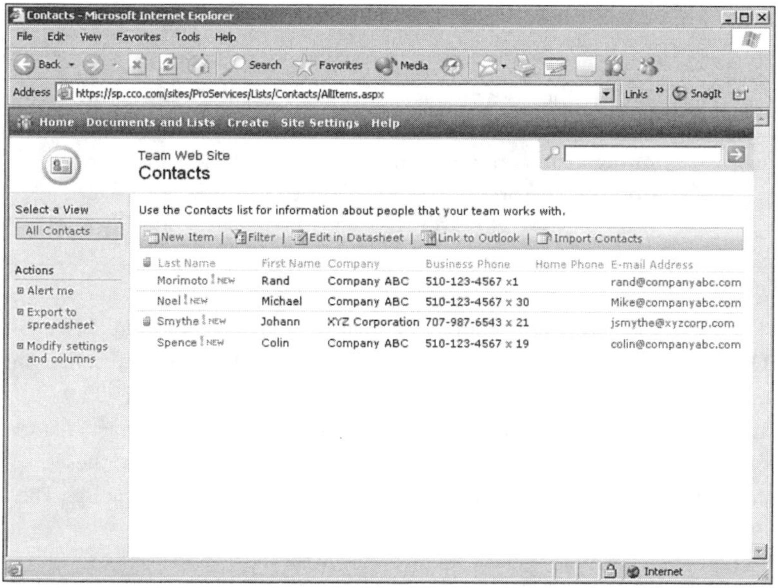

FIGURE 7.2 Contacts AllItems page.

To add a new contact from within the contacts list, click **New Item** and in the New Item page (referenced as NewForm.aspx in the URL) add the information as prompted. The contact's last name is mandatory, but the other items are optional. Obviously, first name, email address, business phone, mobile phone, and address are generally useful to have. A web page can be added for a contact, which could be a company site if the contact works for a different company, or departmental site, if the contact is in a different department. Some organizations will store resumes in a SharePoint folder and provide a link to the individual's resume in a contacts list.

In the toolbar on the New Item page the option is given to attach a file. This can be used to attach a resume as well, or you could attach a picture of the individual. In Figure 7.2 the entry of Johann Smythe has a paperclip icon next to it, indicating an attached file. Clicking the paperclip icon doesn't actually open the attachment; you need to click the last name (which opens up the DispForm.aspx page, showing all the information entered about that contact), scroll down to the attachment name, and then click it. This page also tells you who created the contact and when, and who last edited it and when.

> **TIP** If the contacts list doesn't offer all the fields you need, a Site Administrator can add new columns for items such as pager number, birthday, and similar information. Lesson 9, "Introduction to Metadata," covers the process of adding new columns to lists and libraries.

Two other tools available from the toolbar in the contacts list are **Link to Outlook** and **Import Contacts**. You must have Outlook 2000 installed on your desktop to use the Link to Outlook feature, and Outlook 2002 to use Import Contacts. Link to Outlook allows you to export the contacts list to Outlook, where it can be read, but not added to. One or more of these contacts could, however, then be moved to a modifiable contacts list. The

Import Contacts tool allows you to select one or more Outlook contacts to pull into the SharePoint list. These tools can be extremely useful in sharing contact information with users of the site.

The Events List

The events list is also a standard feature on websites created with the Team Site template, as well as in document workspaces. The events list is a bit more complicated than the links and contacts lists because events are typically viewed in a calendar format as opposed to a list of dates and times— which can be confusing to figure out. Most SharePoint users are also familiar with the Outlook calendar and expect this presentation.

Figure 7.3 shows a portion of the New Item page (referenced as NewForm.apsx in the URL), accessible by clicking **Add new event** from the events Web Part on the site home page, or from within the events list (referenced as AllItems.aspx in the URL). A title must be entered for each event, as well as a beginning time. A description and location are optional. In this example, a recurring event is being created, and in Figure 7.3 in the Recurrence section, the circle is filled next to Weekly, which brings up the recurrence options shown in the bottom half of the figure. These options are fairly self-explanatory, but note that recurring events can take place on several days in a week, not just one. Make sure you specify a start date (or click the calendar icon and use the pop-up calendar to choose the date) and either select **No end date**, enter a number of occurrences, or enter an end date. In this case, the event happens every Monday, Wednesday, and Friday and ends on 12/4/04.

At the bottom of the New Item page is the option to create a meeting workspace for this event. Meeting workspaces were discussed in Lesson 3, "SharePoint Site Collections Demystified," and are web pages in SharePoint dedicated to storing and managing information pertinent to a specific event. A file can also be attached to the event (for example, an agenda), and this often will suffice, and it isn't necessary to then create a dedicated meeting workspace. The new event is then created by clicking on **Save and Close**.

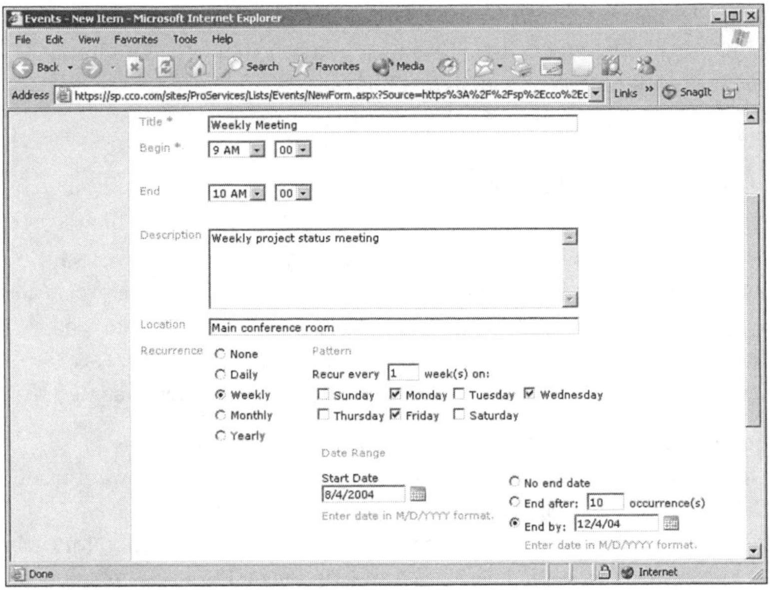

FIGURE 7.3 Creating a recurring event.

The Calendar View of the Events List

Figure 7.4 shows the calendar view of the events list after the recurring event has been added in the previous section. This view can be accessed by opening the events Web Part from the home page and then clicking the Calendar view. Note in this example that the weekly meeting appears on every day and is underlined. Clicking the event name will open the event (referenced asDispForm.aspx in the URL) and show the details of the event.

In the toolbar, you are given the options **New Item, Link to Outlook, Today, View by Day, View by Week,** and **View by Month**. Figure 7.4 shows the monthly view, and you can see the following or previous month's events by clicking the arrow to the left or right of the month name. The **Link to Outlook** feature exports the information contained in the events list to Outlook as read-only information that is updated as the events list changes.

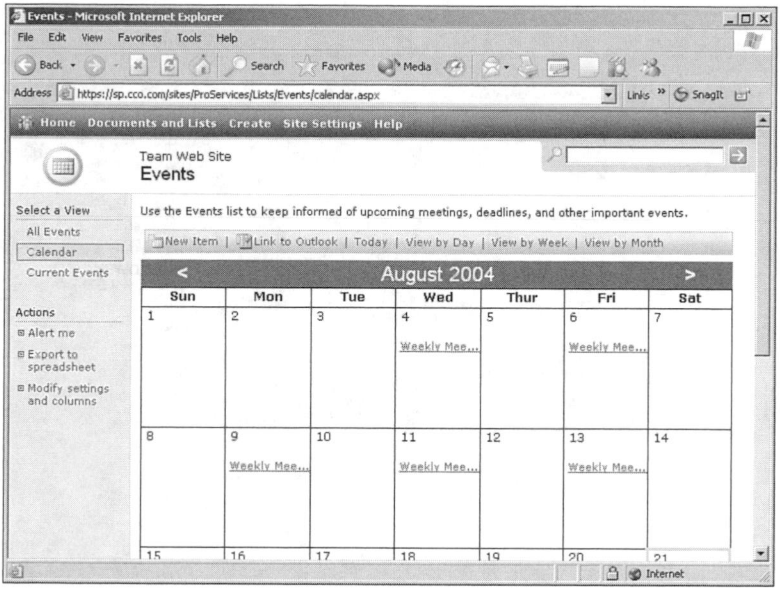

FIGURE 7.4 Calendar view in the events list.

TIP Searching will take place on the current view only. So if you are looking for an event that contains your name, for example, only the current view will be searched. If you have the calendar view selected with View by Month chosen, only the month currently shown will be searched. For more effective searching, you are better off in the All Events view.

Selecting the Calendar View from the Home Page

The outlined Web Part in Figure 7.5 shows the less-than-ideal view from the home page after the recurring event has been added. Most users agree this is not a very helpful way to see upcoming events, because they are used to seeing a calendar view.

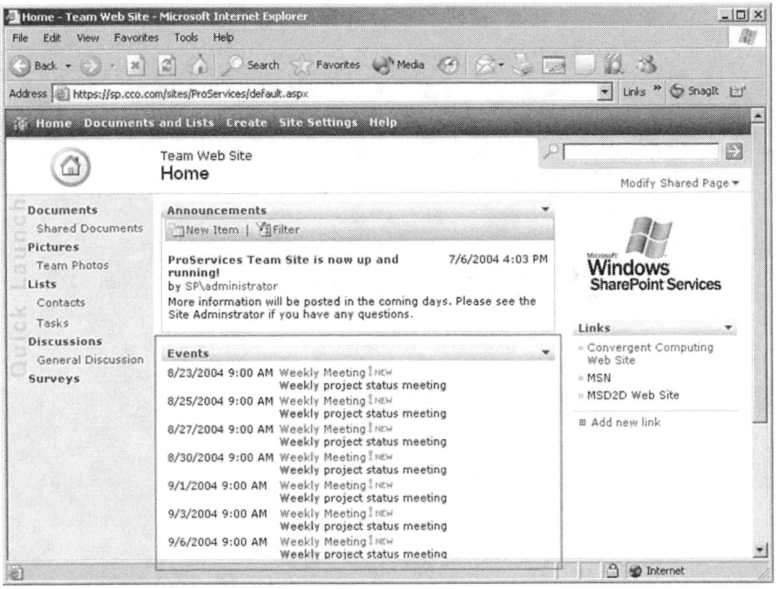

FIGURE 7.5 Events list showing all events on the home page.

To rectify this problem, you (or a Site Administrator) can follow these steps:

1. From the site home page, where the events Web Part is visible, click the black down arrow in the Events title bar.

2. Click **Modify Shared Web Part**.

3. In the List Views section under Selected View is a drop-down menu field, which by default will have Current View selected. Click the down arrow and select **Calendar**.

4. A warning message will come up informing you that you may disable Web Part connections, so only make the change if you are sure there aren't Web Part connections to this list in place. Click **OK**.

5. Click **OK** again. You'll see a display similar to what's shown in Figure 7.6, which most users agree is easier to read than the display in Figure 7.5.

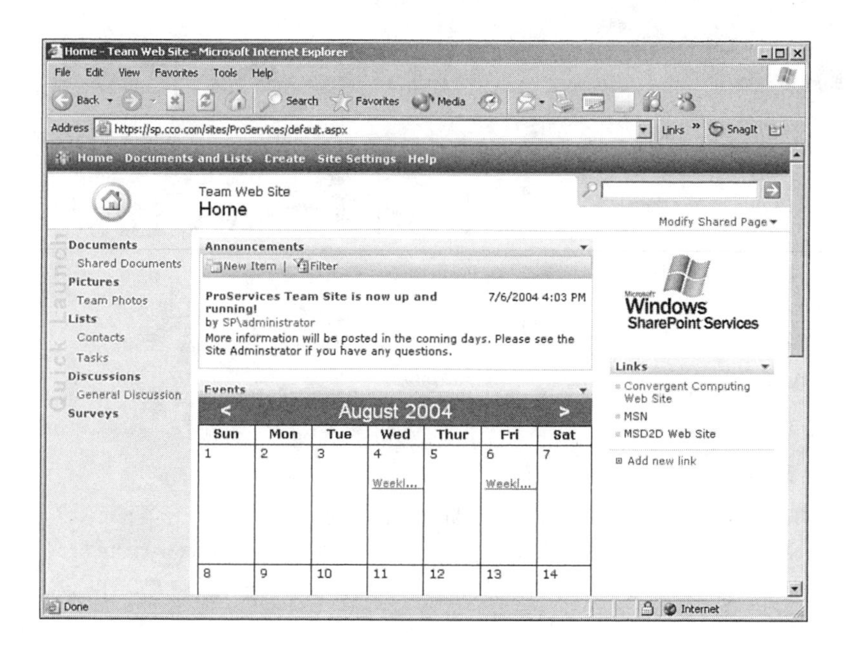

FIGURE 7.6 Events list with calendar view on the home page.

Summary

This lesson provided an overview of the features and capabilities of the links, contacts, and events lists in SharePoint. These lists are quite straightforward, and most users understand their purposes right away. Some more advanced tools can be used to import and export contacts to and from the contacts list and can be used to export events from the events list. The events list is typically most useful when the calendar view is used from the AllItems.aspx page and when the calendar view is selected to be displayed on the home page.

LESSON 8
Using the Tasks and Issues Lists

In this lesson we will examine the tasks and issues lists—both extremely useful, but complex standard Web Parts.

The Tasks List

The tasks list is offered as a standard feature of SharePoint sites created using the Team Site template, as well as of a document workspace and decision meeting workspaces. This Web Part is well-suited for managing tasks within a project or departmental site.

Figure 8.1 shows a sample tasks list with four items in it. All four of these items happen to pertain to a sample project called the SMS Project. The All Tasks view is the default view, and it organizes the entries based on the ID number that SharePoint assigns to items added to this list. The All Tasks view includes a number of standard columns of information: attachments (the paperclip icon indicates if the task has one or more attachments associated with it), the title of the task, who it is assigned to, the status of the task, the task's priority, its due date, and the percentage complete.

> **TIP** To make this task list more useful, you could add some metadata columns to the list (for example, Client Name, Project Name, and Dependencies). This would make it easier for anyone using the list to be able to find tasks that pertain to a particular client or find a specific project type or name. Also, the Dependencies column could show whether a preceding item needs to be completed before the task can be started. Lesson 9, "Introduction to Metadata," provides information about adding metadata like this to a list.

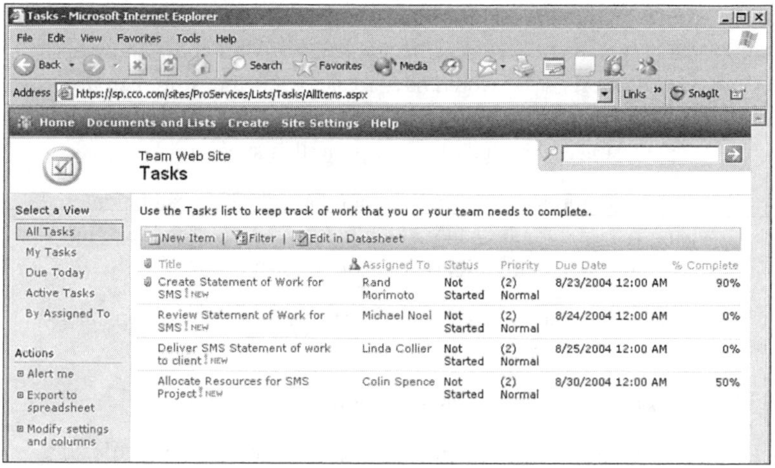

FIGURE 8.1 Sample All Tasks view.

To create a new task, as shown in Figure 8.2, follow these steps:

1. From within the tasks list, click **New Item** from any of the standard views within the tasks list.
2. Enter the title of the task. The title should be meaningful so that a user reading it immediately knows the context. For example, "write document" doesn't convey much information, whereas "write proposal for new widgets for XYZ Company" is specific.
3. Select a priority for the task from the drop-down menu. The defaults are High, Normal, and Low. A Site Administrator can change these to be more granular if needed.
4. Choose the status of the task from the drop-down menu. The standard options are Not Started, In Progress, Completed, Deferred, Waiting on Someone Else. Once again, the Site Administrator can change, add, or remove items on this list.
5. Enter in a percentage complete if the task has been started.
6. From the Assigned To drop-down menu, select the individual to whom the task is assigned. Note that the user needs to be assigned to a site group in the top-level site that contains the task list for that user to show up here. For example, if you want to

assign a task to Bob, but Bob has not been assigned to any of the site groups that have access to the list, he won't show up in the drop-down list. You would have to ask your Site Administrator to add Bob to a site group that has access to the list, or add Bob as a guest user who only has access to that specific list.

7. Enter description information about the task. This can be entered using rich text, and it can include bold and underlined text, numbers, bullets, and highlights for more impact.

8. Enter a start date manually, or select one from the pop-up calendar icon. Enter the start time as well.

9. Enter a due date in the same fashion.

10. Attach a file by clicking **Attach File** (or attach multiple files if Office 2003 is in use on your computer) and then click **Save and Close** in the menu bar.

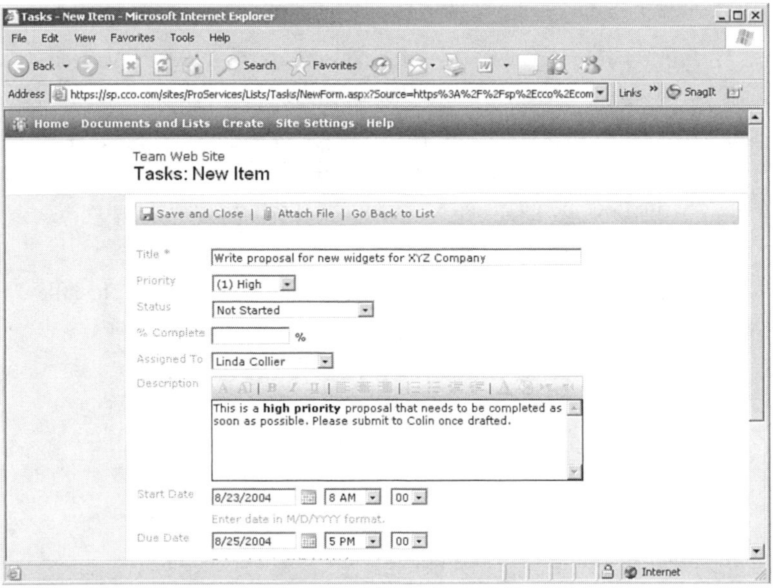

FIGURE 8.2 Adding a new task.

Sorting and Viewing Tasks

Simply click one of the different views in the Select a View area of the menu area on the left, as shown in Figure 8.1. My Tasks only shows the tasks assigned to you (if there are any), whereas Due Today only lists tasks with today's due date. Active Tasks shows all tasks that do not have the status of Completed assigned to them. By Assigned To sorts the tasks based on who they are assigned to in alphabetical order.

You can also simply click a column heading to sort by that item. An arrow appears next to the column title to indicate whether the sort is ascending or descending.

Viewing Attachments

In Figure 8.1, the first task, titled "Create Statement of Work for SMS," has the paperclip icon next to it, signifying one or more attachments. To access the attachments, you can do one of the following:

- Click the task title, and then from the DispForm.aspx page click the attachment filename.
- Click the down-arrow that appears when your mouse hovers over the task name and then select **View Item**. Then, from the task detail page (referenced as DispForm.aspx in the URL), click the attachment filename.

Assuming you have the application used to create the document installed on your workstation, the file will then open.

Viewing Tasks Elsewhere

Many users ask if tasks can be exported to Outlook because they are familiar with Outlook tasks, and they would like to centralize their tasks in Outlook and be able to set reminders. Unfortunately, by default, SharePoint does not offer this capability.

SharePoint tasks do, however, show up in certain Office 2003 applications. Lesson 13, "Using Word with SharePoint," will cover this topic in more detail. The Shared Workspace task pane in Word 2003, Excel 2003, Project

2003, PowerPoint 2003, and Visio 2003 provides access to task information for the site containing the opened document. For example, if a user opens a document contained in a SharePoint document library in one of these applications, the Shared Workspace task pane provides the Tasks tab, which displays the different tasks managed by the site that houses the document.

Issues Lists

The issues list is designed to track issues as opposed to tasks. The difference can be hard to put your finger on because a task might involve dealing with different sorts of issues, and resolving issues might be a task. The main difference between the lists is that the issues list tracks two different items from a tasks list: Category and Add Related Issue.

Figure 8.3 shows the New Item page (referenced as NewForm.aspx in the URL), which looks very similar to the screen shown in Figure 8.2 for the tasks list. The only real difference is that an issue has a Category field and an Add Related Issue field, whereas the task item has the % Complete and Start Date fields.

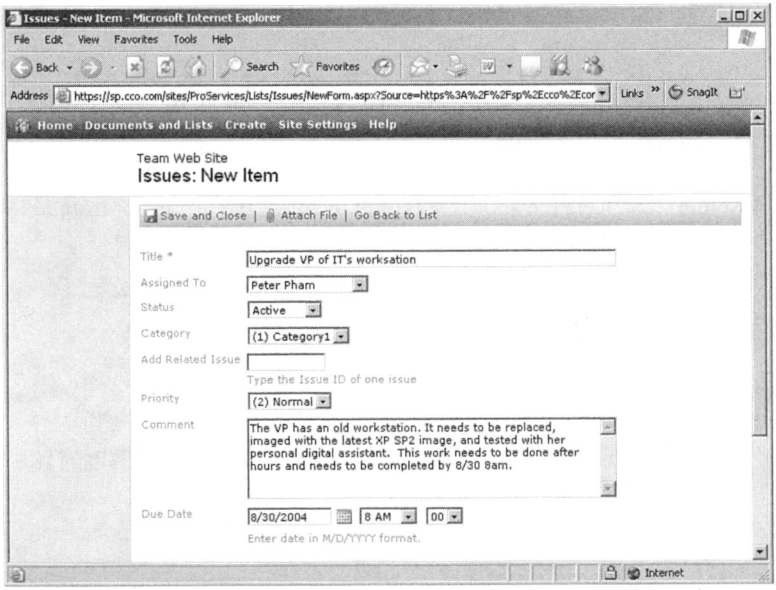

FIGURE 8.3 Adding a new issue.

Figure 8.4 shows a sample issues list (referenced as AllItems.aspx in the URL) with three issues listed. Two additional views are available in the left-hand menu, both of which are self-explanatory: My Issues and Active Issues. Issue 1 has been resolved, as you can see from the entry in the Status column, whereas issues 2 and 6 are still active. Note that issues 3, 4, and 5 are missing. They didn't magically disappear, and they weren't deleted. Modifications were made to issues 1 and 2 before a new issue was added, and SharePoint tracks each change by assigning a new number in the background, which made 6 the next available ID number when the **Schedule additional SharePoint training for end users** issue was added.

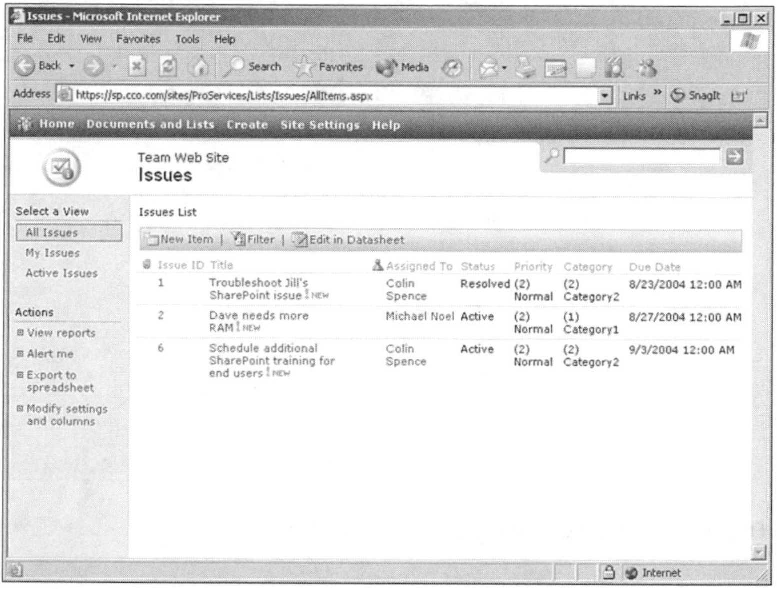

FIGURE 8.4 All Issues view of an issues list.

Differences Between Tasks Lists and Issues Lists

A primary difference between the issues and tasks lists is that the issues list tracks the comments added to issues as they are worked on and makes them accessible to site users who want to view them at a later date.

Figure 8.5 shows the history of issue 1, accessible by clicking the title of the issue or by hovering the mouse over the title of the issue, clicking the down arrow, and selecting **View Item**. The View Item page (referenced as DispForm.aspx in the URL) shows the details of the issue, when it was created, and when last modified, as well as a related issue (issue 6 in the example) and the issue history, which captures the comments entered when the issue was edited and time stamps the comments.

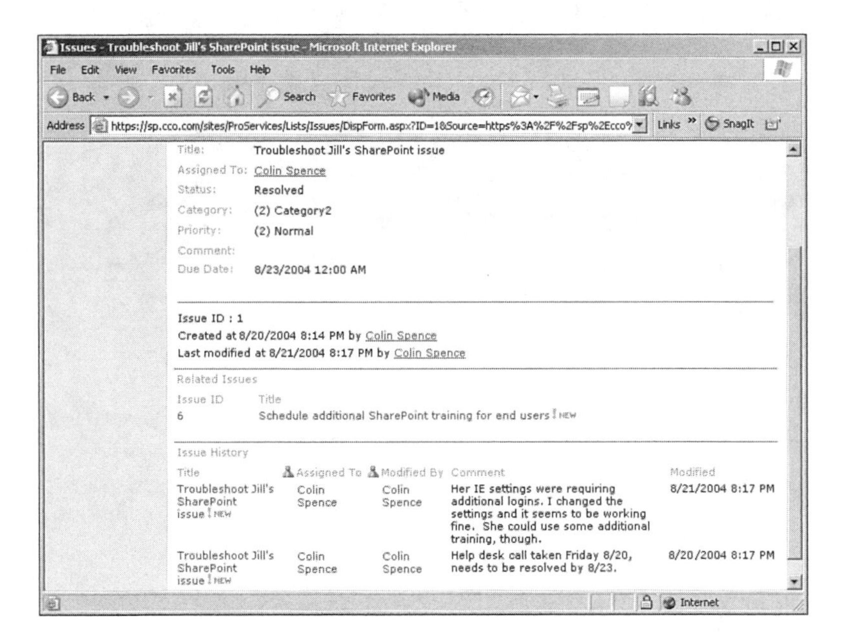

FIGURE 8.5 View of issue details and history.

The issues list also has a handy feature that, when activated by the Site Administrator (available by accessing **Modify settings and columns**, **Change general settings** and then setting **Email Notification** to **Yes**), sends an email to the individual to whom the issue is assigned and notifies that person if the issue changes.

Project Management Applications of Tasks and Issues Lists

Project managers and team leads tend to get excited by the idea of using the tasks and issues lists for assigning tasks to members of their team and tracking them in SharePoint. When properly understood, these lists can be helpful, but a couple points should be made first. Although tasks lists can be used to assign tasks to specific individuals, those individuals are not alerted unless they have alerts set up within the list or are actively keeping an eye on the tasks assigned to them when they are using an Office 2003 application that has the Shared Workspace task pane in it, paying attention to the Tasks tab in particular. There also isn't a way "out of the box" to link SharePoint tasks to Outlook tasks, which is a commonly asked question.

Overuse of task lists can result in extra work for the user trying to keep up with his or her different tasks. For example, if Susan works with six different departments and is assigned tasks within those six different departments, she will need to visit six different sites on a regular basis to see what tasks she has been assigned. Susan can set alerts within each task list so that she is informed of changes, but this could result in alerts about changes to tasks that she doesn't care about because they aren't assigned to her. She could set alerts on individual tasks to send her an email when those tasks change, but they won't alert her if a new item is added.

Third-party companies offer "roll-up" Web Parts that will find all the tasks from a range of sites and roll them up to a central location and organize them by the person they are assigned to. This can be a good solution for organizations that really want to maximize the use of SharePoint for project management. CorasWorks (www.corasworks.com) is one such company that offers roll-up Web Parts, including "Task Roll-up" and "Calendar Roll-up."

TIP Oddly enough, the issues list may be better suited for tracking tasks, because an issue assigned to a specific user can generate an email informing that user that he or she has been assigned to the issue. When an issue changes, that individual will also be sent an email informing him or her of the change. This can be a better solution for departmental use because users often don't use alerts consistently.

Summary

The tasks list and issues list look quite similar on the surface, and they contain similar information, but they have a number of important differences. A tasks list pushes information to a number of Office 2003 applications in the Shared Workspace task pane when a document stored on the site managing the task list is opened. An issues list is designed to track the comments added to issues as they are worked on, so it's well-suited to keeping historical information. An issues list can also be configured to email the person to whom the issue was assigned. Organizations can customize the lists by adding additional columns of information (metadata) and changing the contents of the standard columns, such as Status, Category, and Priority. A manager should think through the pros and cons of using these lists before relying on them too heavily, however.

LESSON 9
Introduction to Metadata

Metadata is one of the key benefits of having a mature document management system such as SharePoint at your fingertips. This lesson gives an introduction of the topic and shows how it can be useful in document libraries.

Defining Metadata

If you've been working through the lessons in order, you will have come across the term *metadata* a number of times and already have a basic understanding of what it is and why it's important in a SharePoint environment. If this topic is a complete mystery to you, and you have come to this lesson to specifically learn more about it, this lesson gives an overview that will help clarify the topic.

The *SharePoint Portal Server 2003 Administrator's Guide* provides the following definition for metadata:

> "Data about data. For example, the title, subject, author, and size of a file constitute metadata about the file."

All documents have metadata attached to them, regardless of whether SharePoint is in use, that most network users will be familiar with. Of vital importance are certain items such as the title and size of the file as well as the last modified date, which many people use to figure out the latest file in a directory. Essentially, this information helps users to find the file they are looking for and to learn something about the contents of the file without having to open it.

A Microsoft Word 2003 document also has some additional default information that you can attach to the file and view without actually opening the file. From within Microsoft Word 2003, follow these steps:

1. Open an existing document you have ownership of, or create a new one. Access the **File** menu and click **Properties**.
2. From the Properties window, choose the **Summary** tab, and you will see several fields where information can be entered, such as title, subject, author, manager, company, category, keywords, comments, and hyperlink base. There may well be information here that has nothing to do with the document if you used a template created by someone else. The **Custom** tab also contains a number of properties that can have values entered.

Metadata in SharePoint

In Lesson 5, "Document Library Basics," document libraries were introduced, and we looked at a document library on a site called ProServices. Figure 9.1 shows the All Documents view of a sample document library used as an example in Lesson 5, but several changes have been made to the original library. The columns Modified and Modified By have been hidden (see Lesson 11, "Modifying and Creating Views in Libraries and Lists," for instructions on how to do this) since the Site Administrator decided that this information really wasn't that important to display. Instead, he chose to display the standard SharePoint column ID, which displays an automatically assigned number for each document in the library. He also chose to create some new columns in the document library: Document Owner, Client, and Document Status. These column headings are highlighted in the figure. Each of these columns contains metadata—data about the file.

Although the standard Modified column (which tells when the document was last modified) and the Modified By column (which tells which network user made the changes) provide useful information, the point of this sample document library is to share documents that have been delivered to clients and to make it clear who owns these documents (which may be different from who posted a document to the library or who last edited it), which client they are for, and the status of the documents.

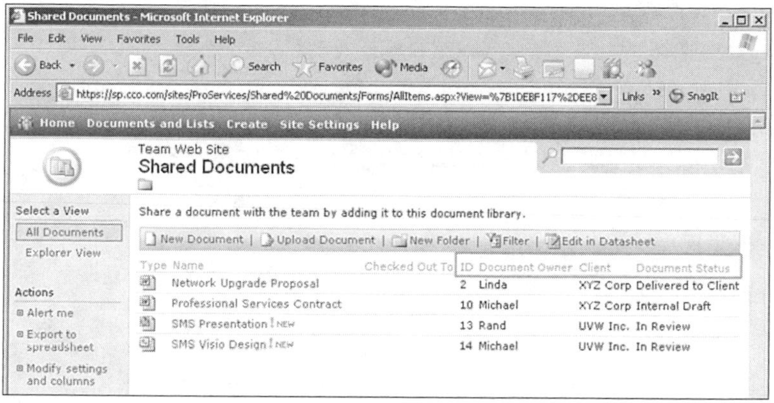

FIGURE 9.1 Metadata columns added to the Shared Documents library.

Figure 9.2 shows the Upload Document page that appears when a user clicks **Upload Document** from within the document library. The numbered items in the figure are the metadata columns added by the Site Administrator.

1. **Document Owner**—This does not have to be someone with rights to the site, because this is simply a text field, so the person uploading the file enters the appropriate information in this field.

2. **Client**—This, too, is a text field, so the information needs to be entered by hand during upload.

3. **Document Status**—This is a drop-down menu, so the user must choose one of the predefined status levels defined by the Site Administrator: Internal Draft, In Review, Delivered to Client, or Approved by Client. Note that the asterisk indicates that this is a required field, so one of these choices must be selected before the upload can be saved.

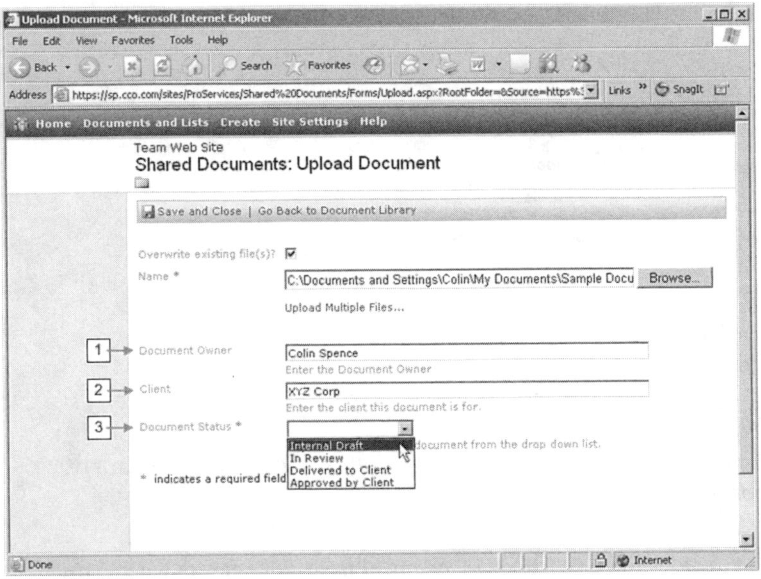

FIGURE 9.2 Metadata fields added to the library.

Different Metadata Possibilities

A helpful way to think about metadata is that each column in the document library is similar to an Excel column, in that the type of information it can contain must be defined when it is created.

If you have rights to do so, from within the document library or list you can click **Modify settings and columns** from the left-hand menu and scroll down to the **Columns** section, which shows the different columns available for editing in the library. Note that the type of information is listed, as highlighted in Figure 9.3, and in this case is either **Single line of text** or **Choice**.

If you have rights to do so, you can click **Add a new column** at the bottom of the **Columns** section and you will see the Add Column page (referenced as fldNew.aspx in the URL), as shown in Figure 9.4. A number of different types of information can be selected, which we will review briefly.

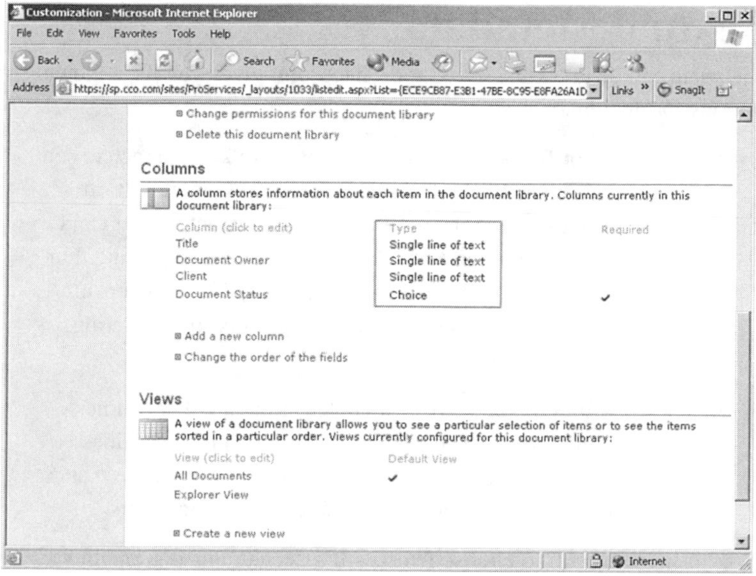

Customization - Microsoft Internet Explorer

File Edit View Favorites Tools Help

Back · Search Favorites Media

Address https://sp.cco.com/sites/ProServices/_layouts/1033/listedit.aspx?List={ECE9CB87-E3B1-47BE-8C95-E8FA26A1D Links » SnagIt

- Change permissions for this document library
- Delete this document library

Columns

A column stores information about each item in the document library. Columns currently in this document library:

Column (click to edit)	Type	Required
Title	Single line of text	
Document Owner	Single line of text	
Client	Single line of text	
Document Status	Choice	✓

- Add a new column
- Change the order of the fields

Views

A view of a document library allows you to see a particular selection of items or to see the items sorted in a particular order. Views currently configured for this document library:

View (click to edit)	Default View
All Documents	✓
Explorer View	

- Create a new view

Internet

FIGURE 9.3 Columns available for editing in the document library.

Create New Column - Microsoft Internet Explorer

File Edit View Favorites Tools Help

Back · Search Favorites Media

Address https://sp.cco.com/sites/ProServices/_layouts/1033/fldNew.aspx?List=%7BECE9CB87%2DE3B1%2D47BE%2D8 Links » SnagIt

Name and Type

Type a name for this column, and select the type of information you want to store in the column.

Column name:

The type of information in this column is:

- Single line of text
- Multiple lines of text
- Choice (menu to choose from)
- Number (1, 1.0, 100)
- Currency ($, ¥, £)
- Date and Time
- Lookup (information already on this site)
- Yes/No (check box)
- Hyperlink or Picture
- Calculated (calculation based on other columns)

Optional Settings for Column

Specify detailed options for the type of information you selected. Show me more information.

Description:

Require that this column contains information:

Yes No

Maximum number of characters:

255

Done Internet

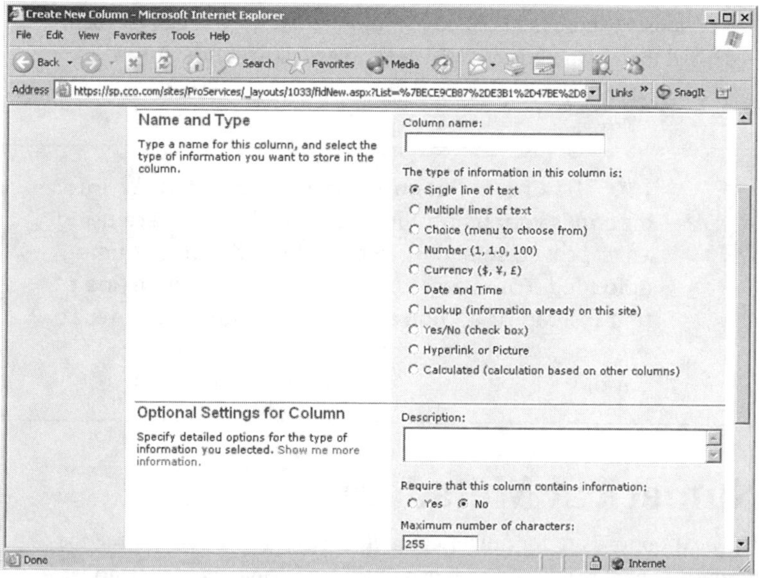

FIGURE 9.4 Add Column page.

Textual Metadata

Metadata can be in textual form, and SharePoint gives you the following options for the input:

- **Single line of text**—One line of text of up to 255 characters can be entered. This helps limit the amount of text entered. It often makes sense to reduce the total number of characters that can be entered based on the kind of information you are expecting. For example, if this column is for a color choice, 25 characters are probably enough, so this setting will stop users from entering long strings of information.
- **Multiple lines of text**—You can enter in the number of lines of text that can be input. The hard limit for the number of lines is 1,000, but it's hard to think of a reason to allow for more than 5 or 10 lines of information to be input, even for comments.
- **Choice (menu to choose from)**—If selected, this option allows you to enter in the choices that will appear in the drop-down menu. Delete the default options and then enter in your choices, with a hard return after each. You can allow users the option of choosing more than one item from the list, or you can let them add their own choice if you select **yes** below **Allow fill-in** choices.

> **TIP** The **Choice (menu to choose from)** type of information is very helpful in ensuring the users are using an approved selection to describe a document being uploaded. For example, if you choose a **Single line of text** instead of a **Choice** field, users can type in whatever they want instead of picking from a list of options.

Numerical Metadata

The next options are for numerical metadata. Excel users will see the similarity here, as in Excel you can define the contents of cells to be numerical as well. These options are also available from the Add Column page (referenced as fldNew.aspx in the URL) shown in Figure 9.4.

- **Number**—You can set the number of decimal places as well as set a minimum and maximum value for this field. If, for example, the field is for a rating system entry, you might limit the minimum value to 1 and the maximum value to 10. You can also perform calculations in this field, which is a more advanced process and won't be covered in this book.
- **Currency**—As with the Number field, you can choose the number of decimal places as well as provide minimum and maximum values. You can also pick the currency format, such as United States, Japan, or United Kingdom.

Other Types of Metadata

Other types of metadata are available as well (as shown in Figure 9.4) and are also available from the Add Column page (referenced as fldNew.aspx in the URL). These are described here, and although some are pretty self-explanatory, such as Date and Time, others require some more explanation and some experimentation to use properly.

- **Date and Time**—You can choose to only have the date entered or the date *and* the time. This field can default to today's date and time, a specific date, or a calculated value (such as 30 days in the future).
- **Lookup (information already on this site)**—This item is a bit tricky. SharePoint provides a list in drop-down format of the lists on the same site from which you can choose information. You then choose from the provided list which column to select information from in the other list. An example of where this is useful would be pulling product part numbers from another list on the same site that contains this information, or pulling information from the contacts list, such as email address.
- **Yes/No (check box)**—If this type of metadata is selected, the user will get a check box when uploading a document or editing a list in Datasheet view. If it is empty it means no, and if it is checked it means yes.

- **Hyperlink or Picture**—Allows you to display a hyperlink to a web page or display an image from the Web. The user enters in a URL. It is then displayed in the library as a URL that can be clicked to take the user to that location, or, if the URL leads to a valid graphic image, the picture will be shown. Note that if a picture is shown, it can't be clicked.
- **Calculated (calculation based on other columns)**—This is the final option shown in Figure 9.4, and it's also a fairly tricky one to master. A simple example is to enter **=Column1+Column2**, which will add the values in columns 1 and 2 and display the value. The *SharePoint Portal Server 2003 Administrator's Guide* provides additional information on this topic (search on "Examples of common formulas").

Importance of Metadata Standards

Rather than "reinventing the wheel" for every document library, it makes sense for the organization to come up with some standards for the different types of libraries that will be used and to encourage different departments, teams, and other groups to use these standards.

For example, in this lesson we looked at a document library in the ProServices site that had additional metadata: Document Owner, Client, and Document Status. A user of this document library might visit another department's site (Marketing, for example) and find a completely different group of metadata added to the document library, which steepens the learning curve for that library. A lack of standards also makes it more likely that users will need help finding what they want, which takes away from the benefits of the document management process.

NOTE From a management standpoint, having the same metadata in two libraries means you can move or copy documents from one to another and the metadata will come across. If there are differences between the two libraries (for example, the column

> titled Client doesn't exist in the new library), the data contained in that column will be lost. It is also possible to create a template document library with all the same metadata so that when someone creates a new document library, he or she can simply choose the template.

It is also important not to overdo the number of metadata columns added to any one library. In the same way that an Excel spreadsheet with too many columns can be hard to read and hard to use, a SharePoint library with too many metadata columns is simply harder to read. More importantly, users uploading documents will be asked to input a great deal of information, which takes time and effort, and they may skip fields, take shortcuts, or simply avoid using the document libraries altogether.

Summary

This lesson provides an overview of what metadata is and how it can be used in a document library. Metadata is not a new concept. It is simply data about data, as discussed in this lesson when we looked at the properties information that can be attached to a Word 2003 file. The document library used as an example here had several new columns added to it to enable users of the library to more easily find the documents they are looking for, and to better manage stores of information. This lesson scratches the surface of the topic of metadata but hopefully makes it less intimidating and gives you some ideas about how to use it productively.

LESSON 10
The Datasheet and Explorer Views

The Datasheet view within a document library or a list offers a number of additional features when compared to the standard view, and the Explorer view has some enhanced capabilities that more advanced users will appreciate.

The Datasheet View

To use the Datasheet view in a library or a list, you must have Excel 2003 installed on your PC. If you click the **Edit in Datasheet** option in the toolbar from within a document library or list, and don't have Excel 2003 installed, you will get an error message saying the list cannot be displayed in Datasheet view.

> **NOTE** Not all list types support the Datasheet view. Discussion boards, Surveys, and Image galleries do not support the Datasheet view.

Figure 10.1 shows the Datasheet view of the document library we were working with in the last lesson. There are four documents in the library, and the Datasheet view displays them and the metadata associated with them in a grid or spreadsheet type of format. Figure 10.1 is scrolled to the right, hiding the left-hand side menu bar, to display the full toolbar. Some new tools are provided in the Datasheet view, as marked by numbers in Figure 10.1.

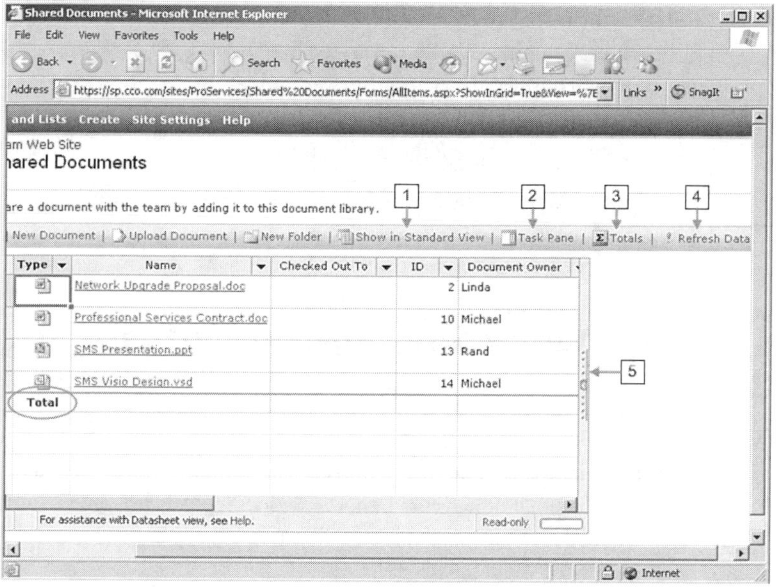

FIGURE 10.1 Datasheet view of a document library.

1. **Show in Standard View**—This tool will change the view back to the standard view.

2. **Task Pane**—This tool reveals the task pane. You can also click the bar indicated by number 5 in Figure 10.1 to reveal the task pane. We will look at the capabilities of the task pane later in this lesson.

3. **Totals**—This tool adds a Total line at the bottom of the datasheet grid area (circled in Figure 10.1) that will automatically add up any numerical information contained in the grid. Note that the contents of the ID column are not totaled because these are numbers assigned to the items by SharePoint, not numerical information entered by users. Instead, if you have a column such as Document Length, where information is entered by the users, the total line would add up those numbers.

4. **Refresh Data**—Clicking this button will request any updates to information contained in the library or list from the SharePoint server. This is useful if several users are updating the library or list at the same time. Clicking the Refresh button in the Internet Explorer toolbar will have the same effect.

5. **Task Pane Bar**—The task pane can also be accessed by clicking the bar indicated by number 5 in Figure 10.1.

Adding New Lines in the Datasheet View

When using the Datasheet view in a document library, you can't create a new row of information by clicking within the datasheet area because a library will only create a new row when a new document is uploaded. Within a Datasheet view of a list, such as a contacts list, a new row can easily be created.

Figure 10.2 shows a contacts list in Datasheet view, and to add a new line you simply click the last line, which is marked by an asterisk, and start entering information. Many users prefer this method of entering information when compared to the process of clicking **New Item** in the standard view and using the resulting interface. As you will see shortly, you can cut and paste recurring information in the Datasheet view, which can make the data-entering process quicker and easier.

Note that in Figure 10.2 the last name Jones was entered, then the first name Bill, and in the Company column, when the letter *c* was typed, the user was given the full company name (Company ABC) as an option. By using the down arrow on the keyboard to select the full name and hitting **Enter**, the user can select this option. Again, this can be a timesaver for entering repetitive information, which Excel users will be used to.

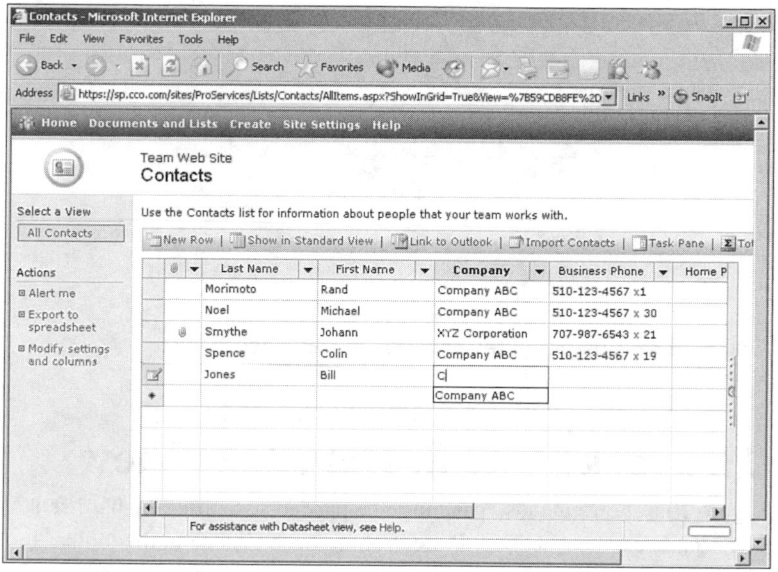

FIGURE 10.2 Adding a new line in the Datasheet view of a list.

Enhanced Filtering

A useful feature of the Datasheet view is the enhanced ability to filter the contents of a library or list by clicking the down arrow at the top of the column next to a column title. When this arrow is clicked, you get the following options: Sort Ascending, Sort Descending, (Show All), (Custom Filter), and then a list of the unique values in the column.

Figure 10.3 shows the results of clicking the down arrow and selecting **(Custom Filter)**. In this example, the comparison operator **equals** was selected, the options **Linda** and **Rand** were selected, with the variable **Or** chosen to define the results. When **OK** is clicked, all documents with Linda or Rand as the document owners are shown. Other comparison operators available are: does not equal, is greater than, is less than, begins with, and contains. This makes the custom filter very useful for long lists to narrow down what is actually displayed.

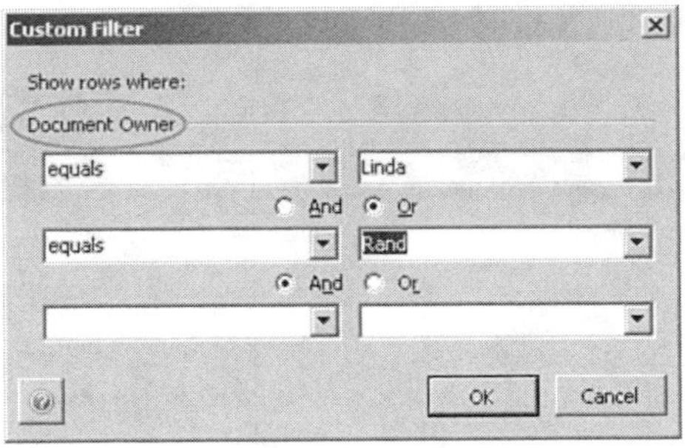

FIGURE 10.3 Custom Filter window in Datasheet view.

The Task Pane in Datasheet View

Figure 10.4 shows the task pane in its expanded state after the bar itself has been clicked or the **Task Pane** tool has been clicked in the toolbar in Datasheet view. A variety of different tools are made available with the task pane. We don't have space to cover each in depth, so we'll discuss the more often used tools. You are encouraged to experiment more with these tools or your own.

1. **Task pane tools**—These include the basic Cut, Copy, and Paste tools, the Undo tool, the Sort tool, Remove Filter/Sort, and Help buttons. These tools are designed for cutting, copying, and pasting cells within a list or between lists. Note that if you cut an entire row in a list, you will get a message stating that you won't be able to undo this Delete operation. Therefore, the Undo tool has limitations. Note also that if you copy multiple cells in one list, there has to be a corresponding set of cells in the second list. So, for example, if you select two cells in the issues list and want to paste into the tasks list, your target cells need to be of compatible data types. If, for example, you try to paste a date/time cell into a lookup cell, you will get the following error: "Cannot paste the copied data due to data type mismatches or invalid data."

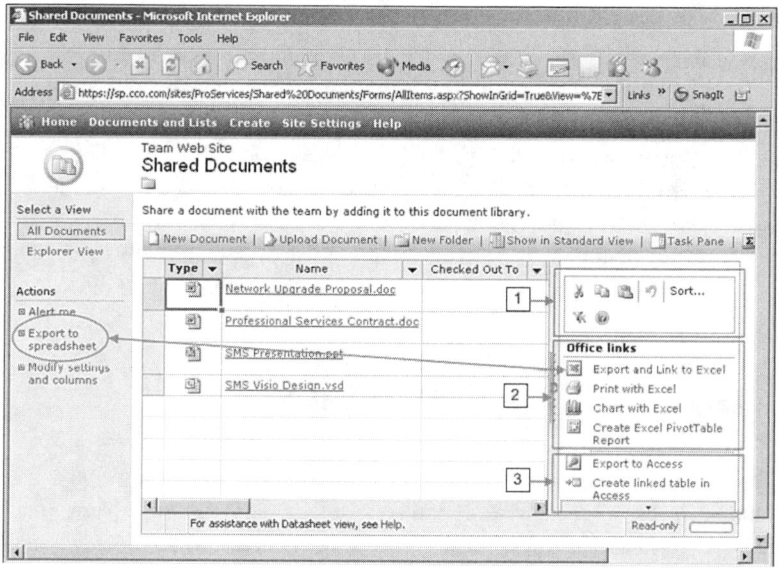

FIGURE 10.4 Task pane in Datasheet view.

2. **Office Links: Excel tools**—Figure 10.4 shows four different Excel tools available: Export and Link to Excel, Print with Excel, Chart with Excel, and Create Excel PivotTable Report. The Export and Link to Excel feature is very useful, and Lesson 14, “Using Excel with SharePoint,” covers this feature in more depth. This tool performs the same function as the Export to Spreadsheet option in the left-hand tool bar (indicated in Figure 10.4 by the long arrow). Essentially, this creates a new Excel spreadsheet and pastes in all the content from the current list. If you click Export and Link to Excel from a document library, you may receive the following warning about restrictions within the new spreadsheet: “You may edit existing document rows, but you may not add or insert additional records, or commit changes to folder information.” To add new documents, you must use the SharePoint tools. The other three tools in this section—printing, charting, and creating pivot tables—also require an Excel spreadsheet to be opened, so several steps are involved in the process.

3. **Office Links: Access tools**—Two of the Access tools are shown in Figure 10.4—Export to Access and Create linked table in Access—and the third, Report with Access, is hidden and can be revealed by clicking the black triangle at the bottom of the task pane. When you click **Export to Access**, you will be asked whether you are creating a new database or adding to an existing one. Some organizations choose to export to Access databases rather than Excel spreadsheets if they have specific needs or if the amount of data that accumulates in the list necessitates it.

Using the Explorer View

The Explorer view has also been mentioned several times in previous lessons. It is available in document libraries and picture libraries only. The option for Explorer view will be made available in the Select a View area on the left-hand side of the window. When you click **Explorer View**, you may get the following warning message: "This page contains both secure and nonsecure items. Do you want to display the nonsecure items?" Click **Yes** if this message appears.

Figure 10.5 shows the Explorer view of the picture library. How this view appears will be affected by your Folder settings in Windows Explorer. Therefore, common tasks may or may not be shown in the Explorer view in the library.

In Figure 10.5, the **Folder Tasks** menu and **Other Places** menu are visible. If these are not visible in your Explorer view you can change the settings from Windows Explorer by following these steps:

1. From within Windows Explorer, click **Tools**, **Folder Options**.
2. On the Folder settings General tab, select **Show common tasks in folders** option. Click **OK**.

If the **Use Windows classic folders** option was chosen on the General tab, you wouldn't see the Folder Tasks and Other Places menus in the Explorer view.

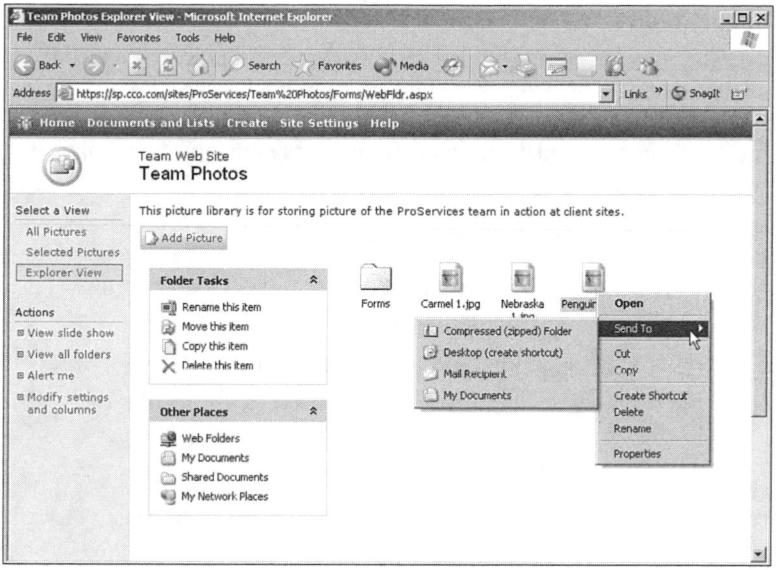

FIGURE 10.5 Explorer view of a picture library.

Figure 10.5 shows another menu and submenu opened by right-clicking the document—which may generate a warning window stating "Running a system command on this item might be unsafe. Do you wish to continue?" (you need to click **Yes**). This menu provides a number of options. Figure 10.5 shows the submenu for the Send To option. You can see that the document can be compressed, a shortcut on the desktop can be created, and the document can be sent to a mail recipient or to My Documents.

Copying Files by Using the Explorer View

The main reason most people use the Explorer view is to move documents from one library to another. As discussed previously in Lesson 5, "Document Library Basics," and Lesson 6, "Picture Library Basics," a SharePoint document library or picture library provides the **Upload a file** or **Add a picture** option in the toolbar. This opens a new window that allows you to browse for one or more documents you want to upload and to enter in metadata information, if the library has metadata columns added. If you use the Explorer view instead, you won't get prompted to add in this metadata, but you will need to add it later. Therefore, using the Explorer view is sort of "cheating" in that you can bypass the requirements of adding metadata information by simply dragging and dropping within this view.

To drag and drop items, follow these steps:

1. Select **Explorer View** from within a document library or picture library. Choose **Yes** if prompted to display nonsecure items.
2. Open **My Computer** and navigate to the folder that contains the file you want to copy. (You can also select multiples files by holding down the **Shift** key while clicking multiple files or by dragging a selection box around these files.)
3. Click the file in Windows Explorer and drag it to the SharePoint Explorer View window and drop the file there. A dialog box will show the copying process.
4. Alternatively, you can right-click the file in Windows Explorer and select **Copy**. Then switch to the Explorer view of the library, right-click in the area containing the documents, click **Yes** on the warning message box that appears, and select **Paste** from the pop-up menu.

CAUTION Notice in Figure 10.5 the Forms folder in the Team Photos picture library. This folder exists in all document libraries and contains the page that SharePoint uses to display the items contained in the library (AllItems.aspx), the page that displays when you are uploading a document (Upload.aspx), the Explorer view ASPX page (WebFldr.aspx), and others. Do not delete any of the files in the Forms folder because the library will no longer be able to provide the functionality of the deleted form!

Summary

This lesson discussed the Datasheet view and the Explorer view and gave examples of some of the tools these views give you access to. The Datasheet view offers tools that Excel users will appreciate, including the Totals option and more advanced filter options, which make it easier to find and display certain subsets of information from longer lists. The task pane is also available in the Datasheet view and offers the Cut, Copy, and Paste tools, which can be very helpful, as well as the Export and Link to Excel feature and the Export to Access feature, which can be very valuable to power users. The Explorer view available in document libraries and picture libraries is a great way to cut, copy, delete, or rename files using a Windows Explorer–type interface. The Explorer view also provides an excellent way to move files from one library to another and to upload a number of files at once.

LESSON 11

Modifying and Creating Views in Libraries and Lists

This lesson delves into the process of modifying and creating views in libraries and lists and how this process can be useful in working with libraries and lists.

Why Are Views Important?

A major component of SharePoint is the database, which stores documents and data. This information is only as useful as the tools that are created to allow users to access the data. A critical part of making this information available is how it can be viewed by SharePoint users.

This lesson focuses on modifying and creating the views within libraries and lists. Each standard list and library in SharePoint comes with several different views when it is created. A document library provides the All Documents and Explorer views, a picture library provides the All Pictures view (with Details, Thumbnails, and Filmstrip options) and the Selected Pictures and Explorer views, and the events list offers All Events, Calendar, and Current Events views. Each view was designed to display the information contained within the list or library in a different way to be of use to the user.

The Modify Settings and Columns Tool

For this example, we'll use a contacts list and create a new view to meet the needs of a particular site. Figure 11.1 shows a sample contacts list with five people listed in it—three from Company ABC and two from

XYZ Corporation. The default All Contacts view shows seven columns of information. If you were to add a new contact to this list, however, you could enter in as many as 17 different fields of information, so only a subset of the information that SharePoint contains about these individuals is actually being displayed.

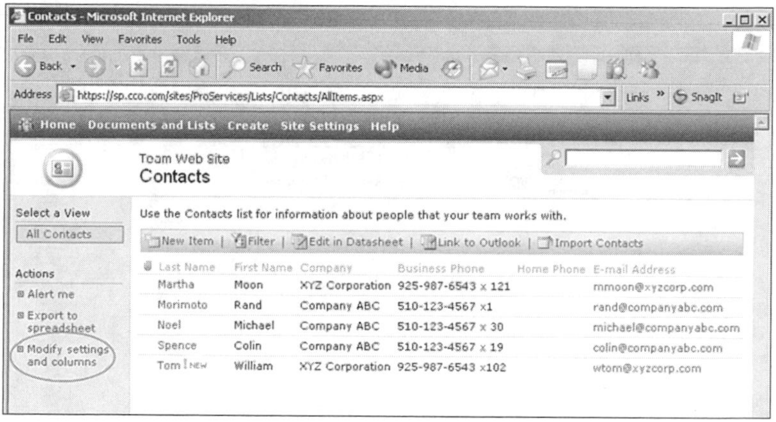

FIGURE 11.1 Sample All Contacts view of a contacts list.

In this example, the Site Administrator wants to modify the All Contacts view to display different information. She has decided that the Attachments column won't be used very often, if at all, and therefore will remove that from this view. She has also decided that the Home Phone column won't be used either, but she does want to display the Cellular Phone column.

To make these changes (assuming you have the appropriate rights), follow these steps:

1. From within the contact list, click **Modify settings and columns** (circled in Figure 11.1).

2. The Customize page (referenced as listedit.aspx in the URL) will open. Scroll down to the Views section at the bottom. Click **All Contacts**.

3. The Edit View page (referenced as ViewEdit.aspx in the URL) will open. Note that the view name can be edited on this page, and the ASPX filename can also be modified.

4. Scroll down so that the Columns information is all visible; this is where the changes will be made. Uncheck the **Attachments** and **Home Phone** boxes and then check the **Mobile Phone** box, as shown in Figure 11.2. Change the number next to Mobile Phone to 6. This means that it will display after Business Phone and before E-mail Address.

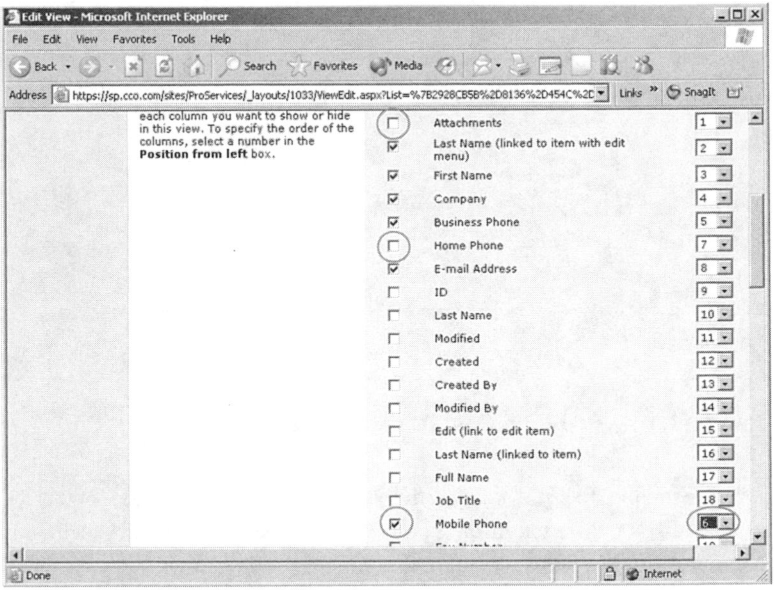

FIGURE 11.2 Selecting the columns to view.

5. Scroll down to the Style section and click the plus sign to expand the section. Choose **Shaded** for the view style.
6. Scroll all the way to the bottom of the page and click **OK**.
7. From the Customize Contacts page, click **Go Back to "Contacts"** above General Settings, and the results will look like what's shown in Figure 11.3. Note that the Attachments column (signified by the paperclip icon) and the Home Phone column are no longer visible, and the Mobile Phone column now comes before the E-mail Address column. Note that the shaded view style shades every other line to make the list slightly easier to read.

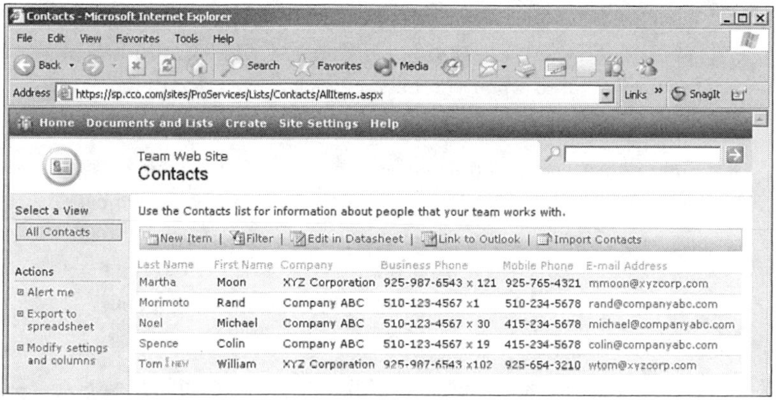

FIGURE 11.3 Results of modifying the All Contacts view.

This is an example of the way an existing view can be modified. Next, we will delve a bit deeper into the options for creating a new view.

Creating a New View in the Contacts List

A new view is usually created once the existing views have been fine-tuned and the Site Administrator realizes a need for one or more additional views for specific users. In the case of this example, the Site Administrator realizes that many of the people using this list will want to contact people who are not part of the organization (Company ABC) . Therefore, a new view will be created, called External Contacts, and a filter will be applied so that Company ABC employees are not included.

For this example, take the following steps:

1. From within the contact list, click **Modify settings and columns**.
2. The Customize page (referenced as listedit.aspx in the URL) will open. Scroll down to the Views section at the bottom of the page. Click **Create a new view**.

3. The Create View page opens, and you are given the options for a standard view, Datasheet view, or Calendar view (Calendar view can only be used when you have dates associated with the items in the list). In this example, a standard view will be created.

4. Enter a view name in the Create View page (referenced as ViewNew.aspx in the URL). In this case, the view will be called **External Contacts**. You can make this the default view by clicking the box beneath **View Name**. In this case, the External Contacts view will not be the default view, so the box is not checked.

   Decide whether this new view will be a personal view or a public view. A personal view will only be offered to you, whereas a public view will be offered to anyone visiting the list. In this case, a public view will be used, so make sure **Create a Public View** is selected.

   In the Columns section, no changes will be made for this view because the Site Administrator wants the same columns to be displayed.

5. Scroll down to the Sort section and select **Last Name** under **First sort by column**. Leave the default setting **Show items in ascending order** checked.

6. Scroll down to the Filter section, as shown in Figure 11.4, and make sure the circle next to **Show items only when the following is true** is filled. Then, under **Show the items when column**, choose **Company** from the top drop-down menu and select **is not equal to** from the second drop-down menu. Type in **Company ABC** (or the appropriate entry for your list) in the third field.

7. Scroll down to Style, expand it and choose **Newsletter**.

8. Scroll down to the bottom of the screen and click **OK**.

9. From the Customize page, click **Go Back to "Contacts"** (or the name of your contacts list) above General Settings and then click the new view **External Contacts**. The results will look like what's shown in Figure 11.5.

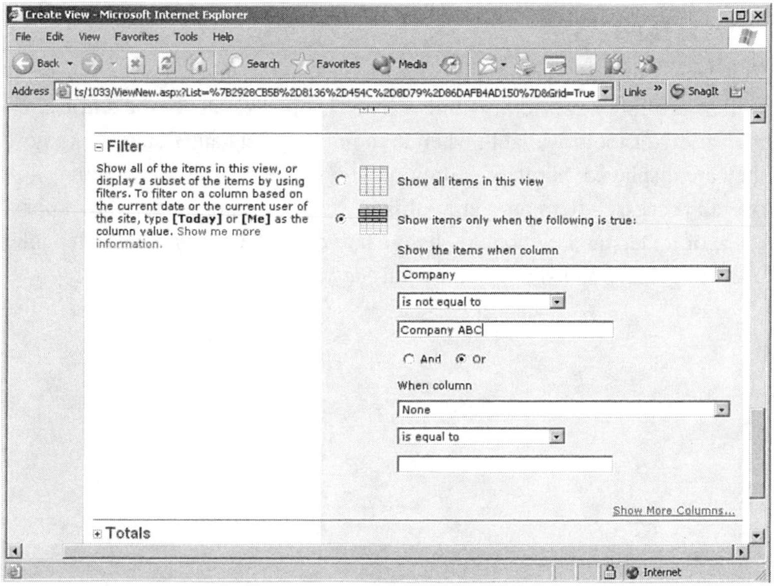

FIGURE 11.4 Creating a filter in a new view.

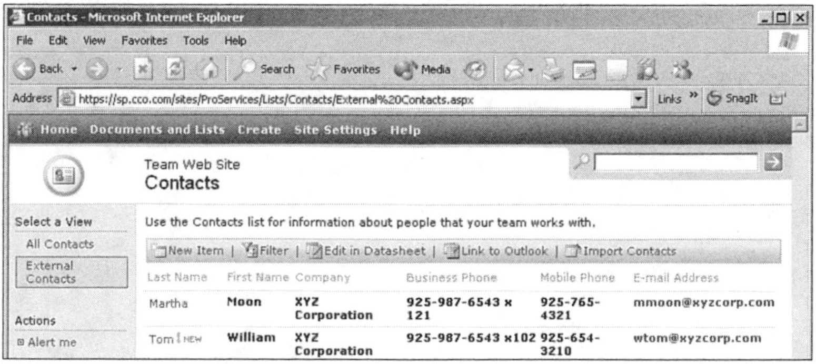

FIGURE 11.5 The External Contacts view.

Now, when a user accesses the contacts list used in this example, two views are available. These views have self-explanatory titles: All Contacts and External Contacts. The External Contacts view only shows contacts who are not employees of Company ABC, and the style is slightly different from the All Contacts view to help differentiate the two views.

Summary

This lesson focused on the process of modifying a view within a list as well as creating new views within a list. This just scratches the surface of the variety of tools available when creating new lists and determining how they are displayed, but it does provide you with the basic steps in the overall process. After completing this lesson, you can now see the importance of understanding how to change and create views of a list, to enable users to quickly and simply find what they are looking for.

LESSON 12

Alerts and Document Versioning

The alert is a very powerful feature that informs users of changes to documents, lists, or libraries; whereas document versioning enables a document library or picture library to retain previous versions of documents.

The Importance of Being Alerted

Alerts add a new dimension to the file storage process, and they allow the files to essentially talk to the users, letting them know when something has changed. This is a dramatic advantage that SharePoint brings to the table when compared to a standard file storage system, such as a network file server or a traditional database. These systems are passive by nature and require the user to go and find, or try to find, the information they need.

Most users have probably experienced the situation where they look in a shared folder on a shared directory to try to find the Word document they worked on several weeks ago. For example, this might be a policy document called "New Policy for Human Resources." When they arrive at the folder, they find 10 different versions of the document, the newest of which is only days old. The dismayed user then needs to open the newest document to try to figure out what, if anything, has changed and who made the changes. SharePoint adds a feature called *alerting* that enables a user to tag files, libraries, or lists so that an email is sent out when a certain change condition is met, such as when the item is changed or when new items are added to the list or library.

Alerts can also be created on the portal if SharePoint Portal Server 2003 is in use, but these alerts will not be covered in this lesson. This lesson covers alerts generated within site collections in Windows SharePoint Services.

> **NOTE** To send alerts, SharePoint must be configured to communicate to a compatible email system such as Microsoft Exchange. In addition, a user must have the View Items right to sign up for alerts.

Creating an Alert

When you are in a list or library, you will see the option **Alert me** available in the left-hand menu bar (circled in Figure 12.1). This figure shows a sample document library that contains files a departmental manager wants to keep an eye on. The manager wants to know if any new documents are added to this library.

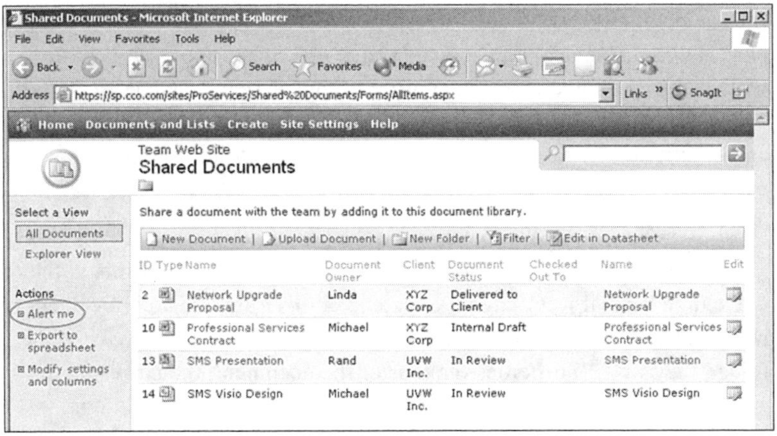

FIGURE 12.1 Alert me option in a document library.

The steps required to do this are as follows:

1. From within a document library, click **Alert me** in the left-hand menu bar (circled in Figure 12.1).

> **NOTE** Note that you can also set an alert on an individual document. From within the document library, hover your mouse over the document name and then select **Alert Me**. This will then take you to the same New Alert page as discussed in step 2, but the alert will be for the document only, not the library.

2. The New Alert page opens (SubNew.aspx), as shown in Figure 12.2. This page shows the email address associated with the user (which is either entered by the Site Administrator or associated with the user account if pulled in from Active Directory).
3. Select the appropriate Change Type setting, which for a library are All changes, Added items, Changed items, Deleted items, and Web discussion updates. (In this example, the manager wants to know of any additions, so **Added items** has been chosen.)
4. Select the Alert Frequency setting from the options provided: Send e-mail immediately, Send a daily summary, and Send a weekly summary. (The manager doesn't want multiple emails each day, so the **Send a daily summary** option has been chosen.)
5. Click **OK** to save the alert.

When a new alert is created, SharePoint will send out a notification email to the user, letting him or her know that the alert has been created. Figure 12.3 shows a sample email that indicates the user has successfully created an alert for the Shared Documents library. The email contains two hyperlinks that can be clicked to go directly to those locations: one for the site itself (Team Web Site) and one for a page that tracks alerts on that site.

Figure 12.4 shows a sample email that arrives when a new document is actually posted to the library. Several hyperlinks are available on this email that are useful to the user. The top hyperlink (number 1 in Figure 12.4) links to the site itself (ProServices in this case). The next hyperlink on the list (number 2) links to the document library, and the third hyperlink (number 3) links to the document itself. The fourth hyperlink (number 4) takes the user to his or her My Alerts page, which gives the user a central place to manage his or her alerts.

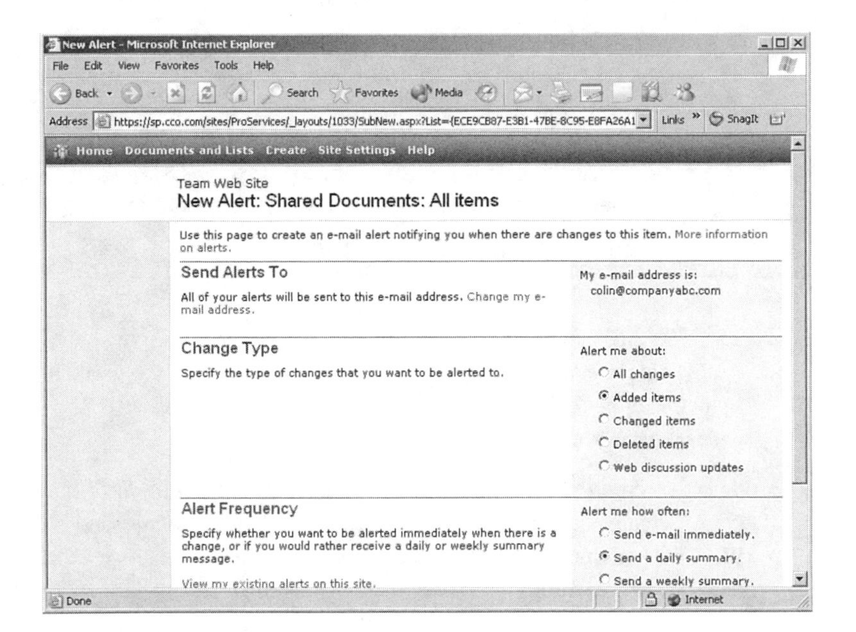

FIGURE 12.2 New Alert options page.

You have successfully created an alert for 'Shared Documents' - Message (HTML)

File Edit View Insert Format Tools Actions Help

Reply | Reply to All | Forward

From: Team Web Site [spadmin@cco.com] Sent: Sun 8/29/2004 5:12 PM
To: Colin Spence
Cc:
Subject: You have successfully created an alert for 'Shared Documents'

An alert has successfully been added on 'Team Web Site' for the item, list, or library 'Shared Documents'.

You will receive alerts in e-mail. The timing and criteria for the alerts depend on the settings entered when the alert was added.

You can change this alert or any of your other alerts on the My Alerts on this Site page.

FIGURE 12.3 Sample alert-creation email.

Figure 12.5 shows the view of a sample My Alerts on this Site page (referenced as MySubs.aspx in the URL). Note that four different alerts are listed in this example. One alert is set for immediate notification, and three others will be compiled into a daily report. Clicking any of the alert names (for example, Tasks: All items) will take you to the Edit Alert page (shown previously in Figure 12.2), where you can change the settings on that alert. Clicking the **Add Alert** button takes you to a page that enables you to choose a list or document library to set an alert on.

Work Plan for Email Solution.doc has been added by SP\administrator - Message (HTML)

File Edit View Insert Format Tools Actions Help

Reply | Reply to All | Forward

From: Team Web Site [spadmin@cco.com] Sent: Sun 8/29/2004 5:16 PM
To: Colin Spence
Cc:
Subject: Work Plan for Email Solution.doc has been added by SP\administrator

Alert result
https://sp.cco.com/sites/ProServices - Team Web Site 1
2
Shared Documents Summary
Work Plan for Email Solution.doc was added by SP\administrator at 8/29/2004 5:11 PM.
3
Go to My Alerts to edit, delete, or view your alerts.
4

FIGURE 12.4 Sample alert email.

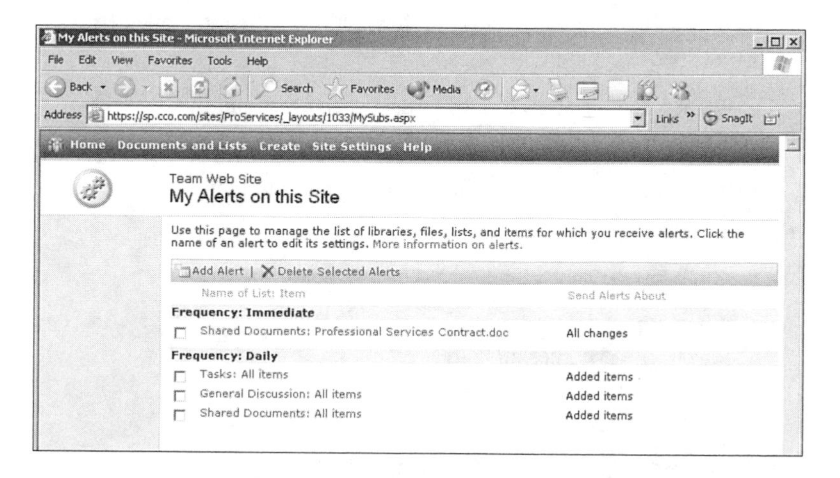

FIGURE 12.5 My Alerts on this Site page.

Document Versioning

Document versioning is another powerful feature that can be configured for document libraries or picture libraries by a Site Administrator. It is off by default, but when this feature is turned on, SharePoint will create a version of the document when changes are made to it. Many organizations prefer this method of tracking changes to documents as opposed to hoping that users will remember to change the document version numbers, add their initials to the documents, or use Word's Track Changes feature.

To enable versioning in a library, follow these steps:

1. From within the library, in the left-hand menu click **Modify settings and columns**.
2. On the Customize Document Library page, click **Change general settings**.
3. On the Document Library Settings page, in the Document Versions section, click **Yes** under the **Create a version each time you edit a file in this document library?** option.
4. Click **OK**.

SharePoint will now create a new version of the document if one of several events occurs:

- When a user checks out a file, makes changes, and then checks the file back in
- When a user opens a file, makes additions, and then saves the file for the first time
- When a user restores an old version of a file
- When a user uploads a file that already exists, in which case the current file becomes an "old" version

Accessing the Versions of a Document

To access the versions of a document, simply enter the document library, hover your mouse over the document title, click the down-arrow, and select **Version History** from the drop-down menu. If versioning isn't enabled, the "Versions saved for [document name]" page (referenced as Versions.aspx in the URL) will state that versions are currently disabled for this document library.

Figure 12.6 shows a sample version history for a document titled Network Upgrade Proposal. Versioning tracks who made the changes, what time the new version of the document was saved, and the size of the document. As this example shows, the document was first posted on 7/5, then a few revisions were made but no comments saved. Then on 9/2 the administrator adjusted some pricing, and shortly thereafter I made some changes to the document and entered in some more complete comments. Comments can be saved to the document when the document is saved after being checked out from the document library.

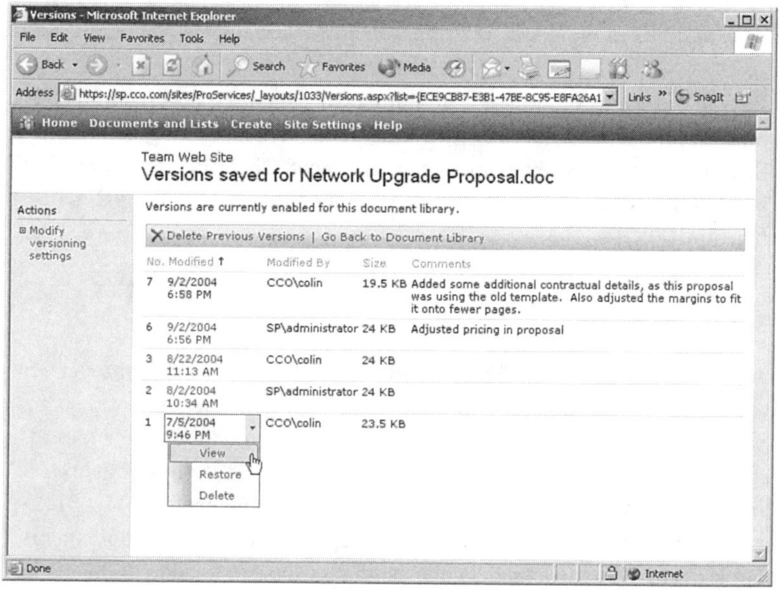

FIGURE 12.6 Versions saved of a document.

Although a detailed analysis of the versioning process won't be provided here, you are encouraged to experiment with viewing, restoring, and deleting different versions of a document.

> **TIP** Without the proper setting, Internet Explorer can make document versioning appear to not be working correctly. To fix this, in IE click **Tools, Internet Options**. Click the **Setting** button in the **Temporary Internet files** section. Make sure that under **Check for new versions of stored pages** the **Every visit to the page** option is selected. Click **OK**. This forces IE to refresh its cache of the page and will correctly display the different versions of the document when **View** is selected.

Bear in mind that versioning can dramatically increase the size of the SharePoint database because each time the document is modified, SharePoint makes a new copy of the document. Therefore, if a document is 100KB in size, each revision, even if only one word is changed, will take up 100KB.

Summary

Alerts are a key feature of SharePoint because they push information pertaining to changes in a list or library or to a specific document to users who request to be updated. Although this takes some time on the part of the user as each alert needs to be created by the user, it allows the user to fine-tune the type and frequency of the alerts. Document versioning is another powerful feature—it not only keeps older versions of documents, but it tracks who made the changes and allows users to add comments if the documents were properly checked out before editing. Document versioning is especially handy because it takes place behind the scenes, so a user accessing the document library sees the latest version of the document in the library, but can access the older versions if needed.

Lesson 13
Using Word with SharePoint

This lesson concentrates on the features offered by Word 2003 when used with a SharePoint document library.

Word 2003 and Office 2003 Product Integration with SharePoint 2003

Many of the documents stored in document libraries in SharePoint will be Microsoft Word documents. Although older versions of Word can be used to edit these documents, using Word 2003 offers the Shared Workspace task pane, which provides a wealth of tools that enhance the connectivity between the document and SharePoint. This task pane is also available in other Office 2003 products, including Excel 2003, PowerPoint 2003, and Visio 2003.

Previous versions of Word can be used, but you will not get the Shared Workspace task pane feature, and some of the additional features discussed in this lesson won't be available. SharePoint is certainly still useful with older versions of Office products, but they won't provide all the same functionality. As mentioned previously, Excel 2003 is needed to use the Datasheet view, and Outlook 2003 allows for the creation of document workspaces and meeting workspaces. Therefore, it is generally recommended that an organization strongly consider upgrading to Office 2003 products to get the most out of SharePoint 2003.

Using Word 2003 to Save Documents to SharePoint

The basic steps of uploading a document to a document library were covered in Lesson 5, "Document Library Basics," but you can also save a document to a SharePoint document library directly from Word 2003. The steps are quite simple:

1. From within the Word 2003 document, click the **File** menu.
2. Click **Save As**. The Save As dialog box will appear.
3. If you have created a My Network Place for the SharePoint site (as discussed in Lesson 2, "Accessing SharePoint Sites"), you can simply click **My Network Places** in the Save As dialog box and then double-click the appropriate Network Place.

   If you don't have a My Network Place created for the SharePoint site, you will need to type in the full path for the site (such as http://spsite/sites/sitename).
4. Double-click the document library to save the document to (for example, Shared Documents in Figure 13.1) and then make sure the filename is correct. Click **Save**.

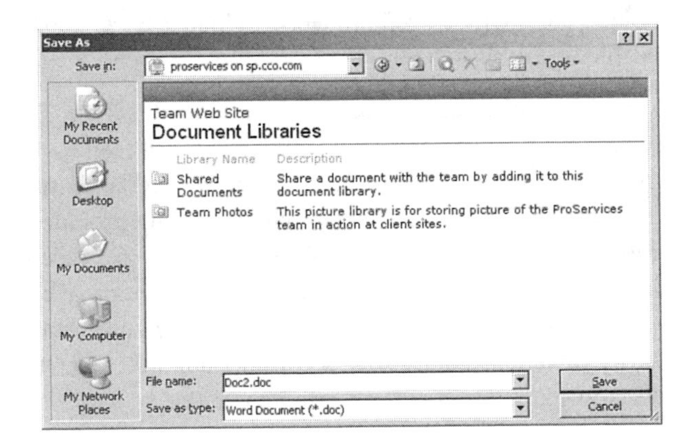

FIGURE 13.1 Save As dialog box from Word 2003.

Opening and Checking Out Documents from a Document Library

Lesson 5 discusses the different ways to access a document stored within a document library. One way is to simply click the document name within the library, which will open it in read-only mode. If the drop-down menu is accessed by hovering the mouse over the document name, the user gets the option to edit in Microsoft Office Word (assuming Word is installed on the workstation), which opens Word and allows the user to work on the document normally.

SharePoint is also designed to allow documents to be "checked out," which locks the file in SharePoint so no one else can edit it. Best practice is for users to check out a document before they click the **Edit in Microsoft Office Word** option. This locks the file and also lets other document library users know that the document is already checked out as well as lists who has the document checked out.

If the document has been checked out and changes are made to it, the user has the ability to check the document back in when he or she closes it, or the user can select **Check In** from the **File** menu in Word 2003. This opens the Check In Comments window, where comments can be entered for that version of the document. If document versioning is turned on for the document library (see Lesson 12, "Alerts and Document Versioning"), these comments can be viewed from the Versions page (Version.aspx) for that document.

The Shared Workspace Task Pane

The Shared Workspace task pane connects the Word document to the SharePoint document library. When a document stored in a SharePoint document library is opened, you should see something similar to Figure 13.2. The six tabs are numbered in the figure. Here's a brief description of the contents of these tabs:

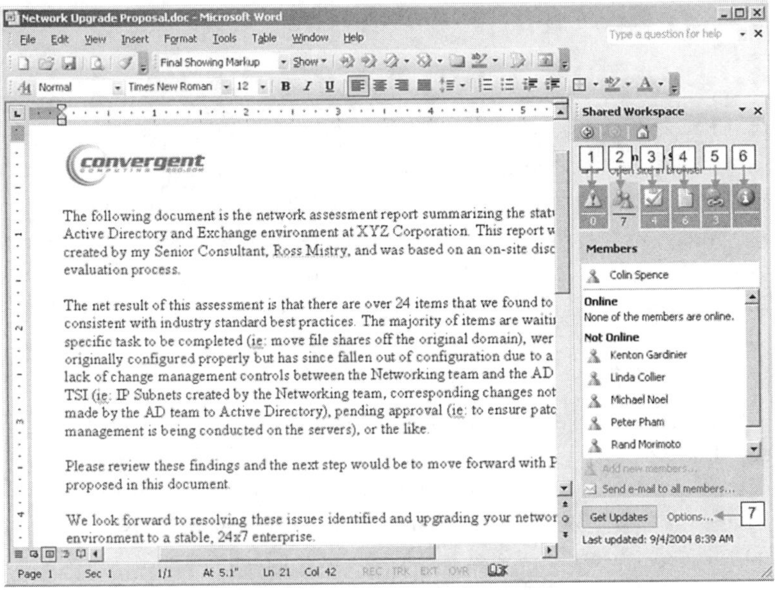

FIGURE 13.2 Shared Workspace task pane in Word 2003.

1. **Status**— Provides errors or restrictions about the file. If the file is checked out, Status will show who has checked it out as well as allow the file to be checked in and allow comments on that version to be added.

2. **Members**—Provides a list of the different members of the site and whether they are online (if instant messaging is enabled on the network). Online status indicates whether the user is available for instant messaging. If network groups have been assigned access to the site, they will show up here as well. Hovering the mouse over a user's name will reveal a drop-down menu that provides a number of tools if Outlook is in use and presence information is configured in SharePoint. These tools include Schedule a meeting, Send Mail, Sign-in to Messenger, and Outlook Properties.

3. **Tasks**—Displays any tasks assigned from the site. The next section will cover the Task tab in more detail.

4. **Documents**—Displays any other documents or folders available in the document library and allows the addition of other documents or folders to the workspace. Alerts can also be set from this tab, as discussed in Lesson 12.

5. **Links**—Displays any URL links available on the site and allows the addition of links. Also, alerts can be configured from this tab.

6. **Document Information**—Displays basic information about the file, such as who created it and who has edited it. This tab allows viewing of version history. If metadata has been attached to the document in SharePoint (see Lesson 9, "Introduction to Metadata"), this information will be displayed here. This tab will be covered in more depth later in the lesson.

The Shared Workspace task pane opens automatically when a document from a SharePoint document library is opened. If you close this task pane and want to find it again, access the **View** menu in Word 2003 and click on **Task Pane**, and the task pane will appear. You may need to click the down arrow in the header of the task pane and then click **Shared Workspace** to properly display it.

> **TIP** You can create a document workspace from within a document that is not part of a document library. When working in Word 2003, select **View, Task Pane**. Then, when the pane opens, click the down arrow in the title bar and select **Shared Workspace** (if it isn't selected already). The Members tab, Tasks tab, Documents tab, or Links tab will prompt you to enter a document workspace name and a location for the new workspace. Then you can create the workspace.

The **Options** button (number 7 in Figure 13.2) enables you to configure when the Shared Workspace task pane is shown, how often updates to the information are retrieved (such as every 10 minutes), and when to save changes to the workspace. It can be helpful to request frequent updates if the documents stored in the library change frequently or the tasks are constantly being updated and you want to be updated more often.

The Features of the Tasks Tab

The Tasks tab (number 3 in Figure 13.2) provides a great way to keep on top of tasks that have been assigned in the tasks list (if there is one) on the site or in workspace in which the document is stored. Figure 13.3 shows the contents of the Tasks tab for the document being worked on. Some of the tasks have check marks in the boxes to their left, and they are grayed out, which means they have been completed. An empty box means a task is listed as not having been started, whereas a black square within the box means the task is in progress.

Note that by simply hovering your mouse over the task name, you cause summary information to pop up that includes the status of the task, who it is assigned to, its priority, its due date, and other information.

Several features are also numbered in Figure 13.3:

1. If the user clicks the down arrow, he or she sees the following options: Edit task, Delete task, and Alert me about this task. If **Edit task** is selected, a dialog box opens that allows the user to change the title, status, priority, assigned-to, description, or due-date information. If the **Alert me** option is chosen, the SharePoint New Alert page (SubNew.aspx) opens.

2. If **Add new task** is clicked, a dialog box opens that allows the user to create a new task and enter in status, priority, assigned-to, description, and due-date information.

3. If **Alert me about tasks** is clicked, the SharePoint New Alert page (SubNew.aspx) opens, which allows the user to create a new alert. See Lesson 12 for more information on this topic.

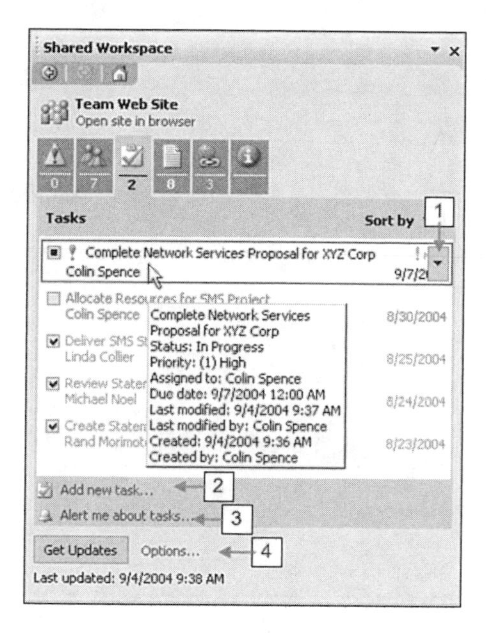

FIGURE 13.3 The Tasks tab in Word 2003.

Document Information Tab

Tab number 6 in Figure 13.2 is the Information tab. Clicking this tab reveals the following information about the document:

- Created by.
- Modified by.
- Modified date and time.
- Document metadata. Metadata was discussed in Lesson 9. It can be added to a document library to attach important information to a document (such as document owner and document status) without changing the content of the document. Figure 13.4 shows an example of metadata displayed in the Information tab.

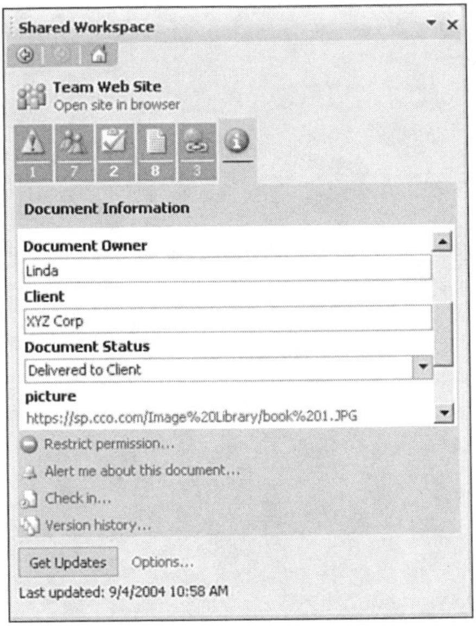

FIGURE 13.4 The Information tab in Word 2003.

So, from the Information tab, the user can see all the metadata columns that have been added in the document library and can actually change this information from the task pane. Note the drop-down menu available in the Document Status field in the task pane in Figure 13.4. By clicking the down arrow, you can change the status of the document, and when an update takes place, this information will be pushed back to the SharePoint document library.

Summary

This lesson looked in more depth at how Word 2003 documents can be used with SharePoint. The best practice is to first check out the document in the library and then use the **Edit in Microsoft Office Word** option. This lets other users know the document is reserved for editing by a specific individual. Once a document is opened from a SharePoint document library, the Shared Workspace task pane is made available (in Word 2003). The different tabs in the task pane were covered in this lesson. Hopefully it is clear that a wealth of information is made available to the user. This information can dramatically enhance the user's ability to access other information stored in the SharePoint site as well as enhance the user's communications with other employees.

LESSON 14
Using Excel with SharePoint

Excel 2003 integrates in a number of ways with SharePoint and can be used to enhance the features offered by SharePoint lists.

Standard Uses for Excel 2003

Using Excel 2003 with SharePoint enables users to access a variety of additional features and tools that many consider to be essential for day-to-day activities. For example, document libraries and lists give the option **Export to Spreadsheet** in the left-hand menu bar, but this only works if Excel 2003 is in use. Also, as mentioned in Lesson 10, "The Datasheet and Explorer Views," a number of different tools are available to the user in the Datasheet view, which provides a spreadsheet-like working environment that can be very helpful when working with more complex lists and libraries. Once again, the Datasheet view is only available if Excel 2003 is in use.

Excel 2003 also can be of great assistance with a number of other standard tasks:

- Printing list and library information
- Graphing data in meaningful fashions and creating PivotTables
- Facilitating data entry

Using Excel for Printing Purposes

SharePoint uses Internet Explorer to display and print content, which severely limits the user's control over printing options. You can't, for example, simply print out the contents of a list because IE will print the page as it displays on the screen, including graphics and menus. Changing the page margins and switching to Landscape view can help, but in many cases there are too many rows and columns of information to show up on the print job.

As mentioned in Lesson 10, the Datasheet view's task pane provides several Excel tools, one of which is Print with Excel. To print a list with Excel you must have Excel 2003 installed and should follow these steps:

1. From within a library or list, click **Edit in Datasheet** on the toolbar to view the list in Datasheet view.
2. Click the **Task Pane** button in the toolbar above the content of the list, or click the right-hand border of the content area to reveal the task pane.
3. Click **Print with Excel**. If the Opening Query window appears, click **Open**, which indicates you trust the source of the file.
4. A new spreadsheet will open, containing the content of the SharePoint list, surrounded by a thick blue line indicating that the range of data is linked to an external source. The Print dialog box will appear as well, allowing you to print the content with just a single click. Alternatively, you can close the Print dialog box and provide some additional formatting.

Figure 14.1 shows the results of following these steps for the tasks list in the ProServices site. The task list was updated with some new tasks, so a total of 14 tasks appear in the list. It is not unusual to see lists that grow to dozens or hundreds of items in production environments. From here you are free to format the content however you like—adding graphics, headers, and footers to the sheet, adding gridlines, and making changes to fonts and colors.

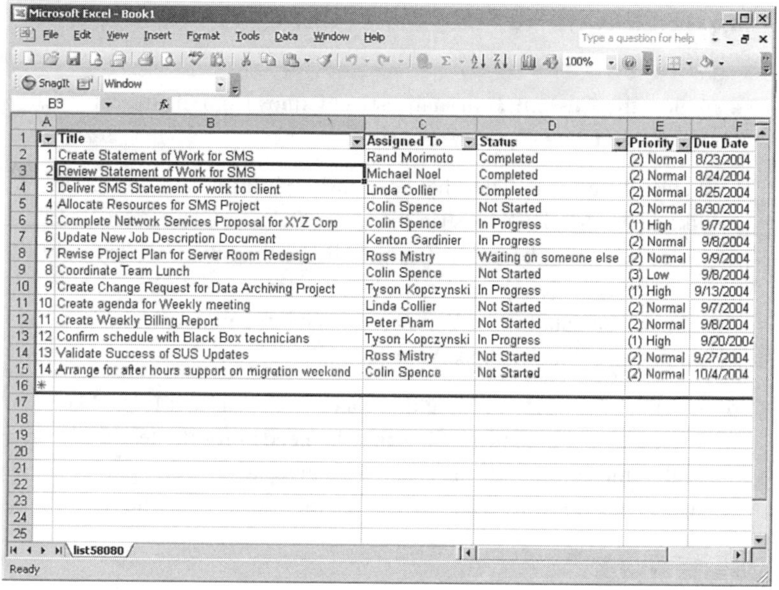

ID	Title	Assigned To	Status	Priority	Due Date
1	Create Statement of Work for SMS	Rand Morimoto	Completed	(2) Normal	8/23/2004
2	Review Statement of Work for SMS	Michael Noel	Completed	(2) Normal	8/24/2004
3	Deliver SMS Statement of work to client	Linda Collier	Completed	(2) Normal	8/25/2004
4	Allocate Resources for SMS Project	Colin Spence	Not Started	(2) Normal	8/30/2004
5	Complete Network Services Proposal for XYZ Corp	Colin Spence	In Progress	(1) High	9/7/2004
6	Update New Job Description Document	Kenton Gardinier	In Progress	(2) Normal	9/8/2004
7	Revise Project Plan for Server Room Redesign	Ross Mistry	Waiting on someone else	(2) Normal	9/9/2004
8	Coordinate Team Lunch	Colin Spence	Not Started	(3) Low	9/8/2004
9	Create Change Request for Data Archiving Project	Tyson Kopczynski	In Progress	(1) High	9/13/2004
10	Create agenda for Weekly meeting	Linda Collier	Not Started	(2) Normal	9/7/2004
11	Create Weekly Billing Report	Peter Pham	Not Started	(2) Normal	9/8/2004
12	Confirm schedule with Black Box technicians	Tyson Kopczynski	In Progress	(1) High	9/20/2004
13	Validate Success of SUS Updates	Ross Mistry	Not Started	(2) Normal	9/27/2004
14	Arrange for after hours support on migration weekend	Colin Spence	Not Started	(2) Normal	10/4/2004

FIGURE 14.1 List content exported to Excel.

Using Excel for Charting

Using Excel for charting is very similar to using Excel for printing. Instead of clicking **Print with Excel** from the task pane in Datasheet view in a library or list, simply click **Chart with Excel**. When the new spreadsheet is created, the Chart Wizard will open to assist you with creating the graph. Typically you won't be able to print the graph you want without some sorting, and it is easier to select the columns to graph before you open the wizard.

For instance, to create a meaningful graph from the example shown in Figure 14.1 of the tasks exported from the tasks list, follow these steps:

1. View the list in Datasheet view and click the **Task Pane** button in the toolbar above the content of the list, or you can click the right-hand border of the content area to reveal the task pane.

2. Click **Chart with Excel**. If the Opening Query window appears, click **Open**, which indicates you trust the source of the file.

3. The **Chart Wizard – Step 1 of 4 – Chart Type** window opens up.

4. Select the **Custom Types** tab. Select **Cones** from the chart types. Click **Next**.

5. Select the column letter that contains the information you would like to use for the X axis (in this case, Column C, the Assigned To column, will be used). Then, while holding the **Ctrl** key down after selecting the first column, select the column that will contain the data for the Y axis (in this case, column G, the % complete column). Click **Next.**

6. Click **Finish**, and you should see a chart appear that looks like Figure 14.2. Some formatting may be needed for the text to fit within the confines of the chart. This gives a compelling and useful picture of who has completed their tasks and who hasn't!

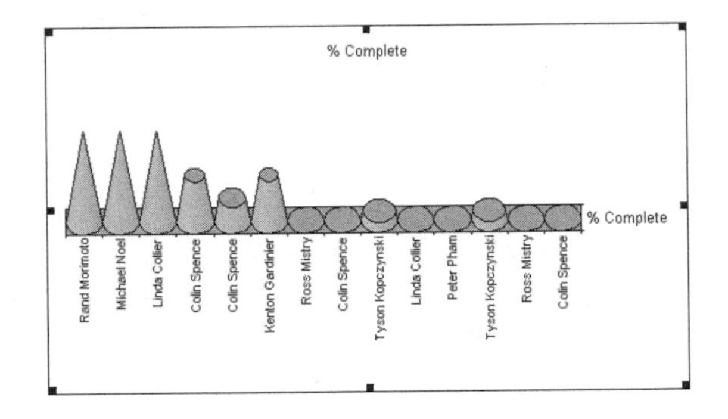

FIGURE 14.2 Cone graph in Excel of list data.

Exporting to Excel 2003 for Ease of Management

We have now looked at two common tasks—exporting to Excel 2003 for printing and exporting to Excel 2003 for graphing. A third common task is simply exporting to Excel 2003 for better data management. As you saw in the previous examples, the Print with Excel and Chart with Excel features start off with a series of steps that actually creates a new Excel 2003 spreadsheet and exports the list content.

Once the data is in Excel, it can be formatted for printing, for charting, or for creating a PivotTable (although we don't have room to discuss PivotTables in depth). The spreadsheet can also be used to enter additional data to the list! Some users prefer to use Excel when working with lists as a mean of entering larger amounts of data.

To create a spreadsheet in Excel 2003 that is linked to SharePoint (and if data is added or changed in the spreadsheet, it can be pushed to the SharePoint list), follow these steps:

1. From within the list, click **Export and Link to Excel** from within the Datasheet task pane.
2. If the Opening Query window appears, click **Open**, which indicates you trust the source of the file.

   If you are then prompted with a pop-up window stating "This list is linked to a SharePoint library…," click **OK**.

   A new spreadsheet opens, with the range of data surrounded by a blue border.
3. Add a new line of data by clicking the last line within the blue border (this won't work if you have exported a library). Enter appropriate text, date, or numerical information or select data from the drop-down menus.
4. When you have entered the information, click **Data** in the menu bar and then select **List**. From the submenu shown in Figure 14.3, select **Synchronize List**, and the data will synchronize with SharePoint.
5. Return to the SharePoint list. Refresh the data by pressing **F5** to verify the data did in fact synchronize.

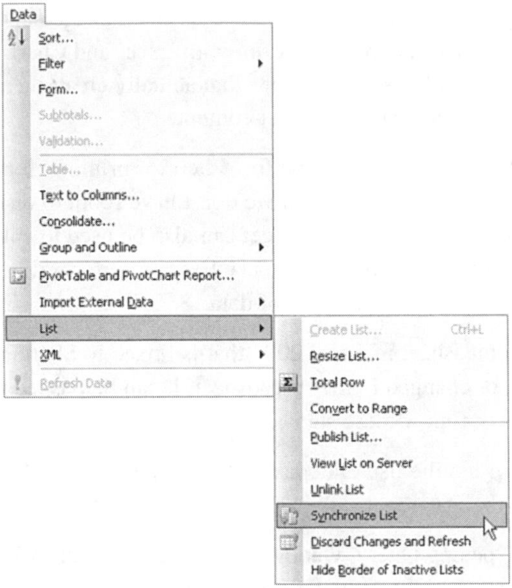

FIGURE 14.3 List submenu in Excel 2003.

Figure 14.3 shows a number of other commands provided when the contents of a list are exported to Excel 2003. The Synchronize List command was used in the previous section. Here are some other commonly used commands:

- **Total Row**—Adds a Total row to the list along the bottom line.
- **Convert to Range**—This operation prevents you from updating the SharePoint list with any changes.
- **Publish List**—This command allows you to publish the list to another location. You will need the rights to create a list on this site. Although this is a good way to publish the data to a new location, the new list won't be connected to the old list or the spreadsheet, so it is like printing the data to a web page.
- **Unlink List**—Breaks the connection with the SharePoint list so that synchronization is not possible.

Saving Your Excel Work

The more time is put into the Excel formatting, the more important it is to save your spreadsheet. Rather than saving it to your local hard drive or to a network folder, you can save your work to a document library on the same site that houses the list you have exported from. Then you can simply open the Excel document and synchronize the changes as discussed previously in this lesson.

This is a great way to export a list (such as the task list we have been working with in this lesson), make changes so the list prints nicely, include a chart in the file, and then save the file to a document library on the site (the ProServices site in this example). This Excel file could then be printed and given to a departmental manager for reporting purposes. A week later, when the task list on SharePoint has gone through a number of changes, you can open the Excel spreadsheet from the document library and synchronize with the SharePoint list so that the spreadsheet and chart are up to date. This time you save back to the document library, and, if versioning is on, you have a nice trail of weekly status reports, with only the latest one visible in the document library.

Summary

This lesson delved into the Print with Excel, Chart with Excel, and Export and Link to Excel features available from within the Datasheet view in a list or library. Export to Excel is available in any document library or list from the left-hand menu bar. Many SharePoint users find that Excel 2003 is essential for printing out reports from lists and libraries and for creating charts. Also, many users actually prefer using a linked spreadsheet to modify and enter data. Having an understanding of this process can be very helpful in getting the most out of lists in SharePoint.

LESSON 15
Summary of the Role of Site Administrator

This lesson summarizes the role and common tasks of the Site Administrator.

Defining the Site Administrator

Before any work can be done in SharePoint, the proper environment must be set up, security must be configured, and maintenance must be performed. In a SharePoint site, this role falls on the shoulders of a Site Administrator. A Site Administrator is responsible for many of the day-to-day tasks required in SharePoint sites. When new document libraries need to be created, SharePoint lists need new columns, and new users need access, the Site Administrator is the one who gets the call.

Each individual site in Windows SharePoint Services and SharePoint Portal Server 2003 is a self-contained environment with its own respective permissions and users. Different SharePoint sites can be set up on the same server with completely different sets of administrators, users, and data. For example, a city government could easily set up different SharePoint sites for the fire department, police department, library, and other branches of the government. Each of these sites would be unique and would only allow the user accounts it contains to access resources. This approach is very flexible because it allows SharePoint sites to be customized to the needs of the individual groups.

When a site is created, the site itself will make the user who created it the first Site Administrator for that particular site. It is up to that administrator to manage the content in the site, add additional users to the site, and control other factors such as search settings and alerts.

Understanding Site Administration Tools

As a Site Administrator, you will need to become very comfortable with the tools available to make necessary changes to the site. Users who are not Site Administrators will not be able to access some of these areas, and for good reason. If a user who does not understand what he or she is doing makes the wrong changes, it can severely impact the site.

CAUTION Remember, SharePoint does not have an "undo" button, so any changes you make are set. This is why it is a good idea to back up your SharePoint site often, especially when you are just getting used to the concept of site administration.

To access the tools you will need to administer your site, perform the following steps:

1. From the Site home page, click the **Site Settings** link at the top of the page.
2. On the next page, you will see three areas: Administration, Customization, and Manage My Information. Click the link under Administration called **Go to Site Administration**.
3. Navigate through some of the links on this page to get a feel for the types of tasks you can do.

Nearly all the administrative tasks specific to your site are located in this area of the site. Portal administration, if you are using the full SharePoint Portal Server product, and cross-site administration will take place in other areas of the portal. For example, Virtual server, antivirus, HTML viewer, and database settings can be configured from a different tool—SharePoint Central Administration.

Administering SharePoint Roles and Rights

Site Administrators are responsible for granting and denying access to a SharePoint site. Unlike with a standard file server, however, permissions to SharePoint information can only be controlled at two levels. The first level is the site level, where access to the site can be controlled by membership in site groups, such as Reader, Contributor, Web Designer, and Administrator. The second layer of administration is at the document library or list level, where Site Administrators can override the site-level permissions that a site group has. For example, in Figure 15.1, you can see that Carrie is a member of the Reader group and that Sophie is a member of the Contributor group for the site.

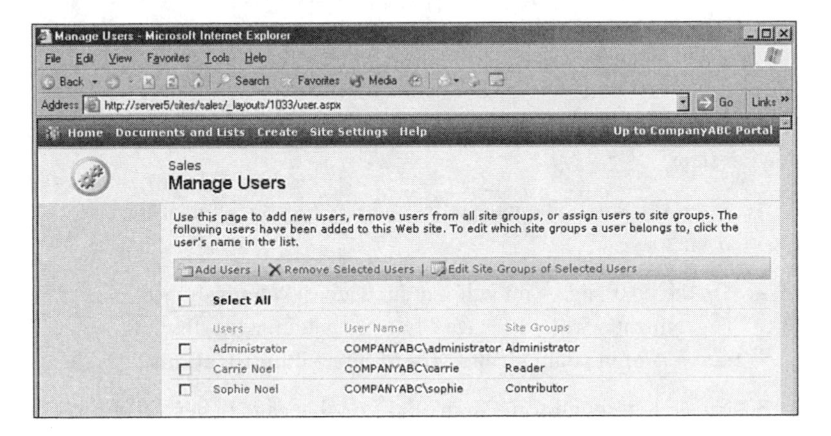

FIGURE 15.1 Setting granular permissions within SharePoint sites.

By default, this would normally mean that Carrie would be able to read all data in the SharePoint site. The Site Administrator however, set permissions at the document library level to only allow Contributors to be able to read information in that particular library. This is a useful concept, because it allows Site Administrators to grant Read access to certain sections of a SharePoint site, while restricting access to sensitive documents in the site. More information on configuring this type of security can be found in Lesson 16, "Managing Site, Library, and List Security."

> **NOTE** By default, when users who do not have access to a site try to view it, they will receive a page that tells them they are restricted and that they can send an email to the Site Administrator, asking to be added to the site. You may or may not want this functionality to be in effect. To toggle this setting, click **Site Settings** from the home page, click **Site Administration,** then click the **Manage access requests** link from the Users and Permissions area of Site Settings. The check box labeled **Allow requests for access** will toggle this setting on and off.

Managing Content in the Site

A site is essentially a big container filled with smaller subcontainers of information. For example, a site may be composed of five document libraries, an announcements list, four custom lists, two discussion groups, and a tasks list. The amount of these subcontainers in a site depends on the needs of the site and how many you as a Site Administrator create.

To administer this information, or to simply get an idea of what is currently there, perform the following steps:

1. From the site home page, click **Site Settings** on the top bar.
2. Under the Customization section, click **Modify Site Content**.
3. Under the Site Content area, like the one shown in Figure 15.2, you will be able to see all the "subcontainers" in your site and any customized ones you created. Customize existing content by clicking the links, or create new content by clicking the **Create new content** button.

A great deal of what a Site Administrator has to do is related to the creation and administration of this site content. For more information on specific types of site content and how to best leverage them, reference Lesson 19, "Creating Libraries and Lists," and Lesson 20, "Creating Custom Lists and Importing Spreadsheets."

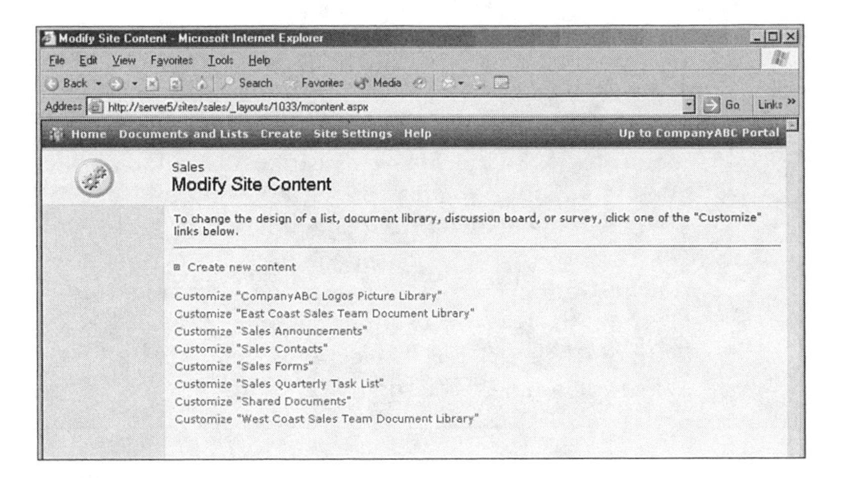

FIGURE 15.2 Viewing site content.

Displaying and Organizing Site Content

One of the main tasks a Site Administrator needs to perform is creating, configuring, and maintaining Web Parts and the overall layout of information in a site. Access to Site Content information is displayed to the users of your site through *Web Parts*, which are components that can be dropped into a SharePoint page to pull information from the Site Content sources and display it in a predetermined way.

Any number of Web Parts can be added or customized to display information in a certain way. Finding the right information to display is an important part of being a Site Administrator. For more information on adding and configuring Web Parts, reference Lesson 18, "Adding and Linking Web Parts."

Supporting and Training SharePoint End Users

A critical component of any SharePoint rollout is training the users of the environment in the use of SharePoint. Using SharePoint is a big shift in thinking for most users, who may be used to the "old" method of accessing files on file servers and via email attachments. It is vital to the success and viability of your SharePoint environment to train the users on the new technology. In general, effective SharePoint training takes one of several forms:

- **Documentation**—Creating a document, preferably with screenshots and step-by-step procedures and guidelines, is one of the easiest ways to disseminate knowledge about SharePoint.
- **Structured classes**—A series of hands-on training classes is one of the most effective approaches to teaching your users how to use the new platform. This type of training can be outsourced to a training company, or you can run your own in-house training. It is vital that the sessions include hands-on practice on test SharePoint sites.
- **Online presentation**—It is becoming more and more easy to produce professional-grade presentations with tools such as Microsoft Producer for PowerPoint. These types of tools allow you to create a web-based multimedia presentation that can demonstrate how to use SharePoint. In addition, the materials can be burned onto a CD-ROM, or placed on a website so that remote users can start to use the system.

Summary

The role of Site Administrator for a SharePoint site cannot be taken lightly. Although it is the responsibility of the Contributors to add and modify information, it is up to the Site Administrator to manage all the access requests and content sources. Once you get the hang of the basics associated with administrating SharePoint, it becomes much easier moving forward.

In addition to the tasks outlined in this chapter, there are many other additional roles that a Site Administrator will likely perform. Many of these roles are presented in the remaining chapters of this book, which focus on specific tasks and procedures that Site Administrators follow.

LESSON 16
Managing Site, Library, and List Security

This lesson covers the process of configuring list- and library-level security. In addition, it covers the topics of security inheritance from parent sites, anonymous access, and the standard Site groups.

Understanding Site Groups

A Site Administrator has full rights to add additional users and groups of users to a site. By doing so, he or she allows those users to have access to the site. The type of access they get is determined by the site group they are added into. By default, Windows SharePoint Services makes use of four standard site groups. These site groups are defined as follows:

- **Reader**—Members of this site group have read-only access to a site. This group is useful when you need to grant a user or a group of users the ability to read, but not modify, information in the site.
- **Contributor**—Members of this site group can add content to document libraries and lists, unless they are explicitly denied access to them. This is a common site group to add average users to when you need them to contribute to the content of a site.
- **Web Designer**—Members of this site group have expanded capabilities, such as the ability to add document libraries, lists, and customize pages to the site. This site group is not used as commonly as the other groups because users are often added as Contributors or Administrators instead.

- **Administrator**—Members of this site group have full, unrestricted access to all aspects of the Portal. Only those users who require this type of access should be added to this group because they can easily view and modify all information in the site. In addition, Administrators have the right to create and delete users and groups of the site.

Adding users to a SharePoint site is a relatively straightforward process. Once you have determined what type of access is required, perform the following steps:

1. From the SharePoint site home page, click **Site Settings**.
2. Under Administration, click **Manage Users**.
3. Click the **Add Users** link.
4. In the Users field, enter in a single user or a group of users. You can specify Active Directory Users or Groups if your SharePoint server is a member of a domain. In addition, you can add multiple users by separating the entries with commas. Enter the users either in DOMAIN\USERNAME format or email address format, such as username@companyname.com.
5. Once you have entered the users, choose which site group you want them to be a member of. In this example, we will choose Contributor, because we want them to be able to add and modify content in the site. Click **Next** to continue.
6. At the following screen, make any corrections or changes to **Step 3: Confirm Users**, which indicates the way you want the users to be displayed in the site. If you have added Active Directory users or groups, SharePoint will automatically add in their info here, as illustrated in Figure 16.1.
7. Under **Step 4: Send E-mail** on the same screen, select whether you want to send users an email to let them know they have been added to the site. You can also add a personalized message here. Click **Finish** when done.

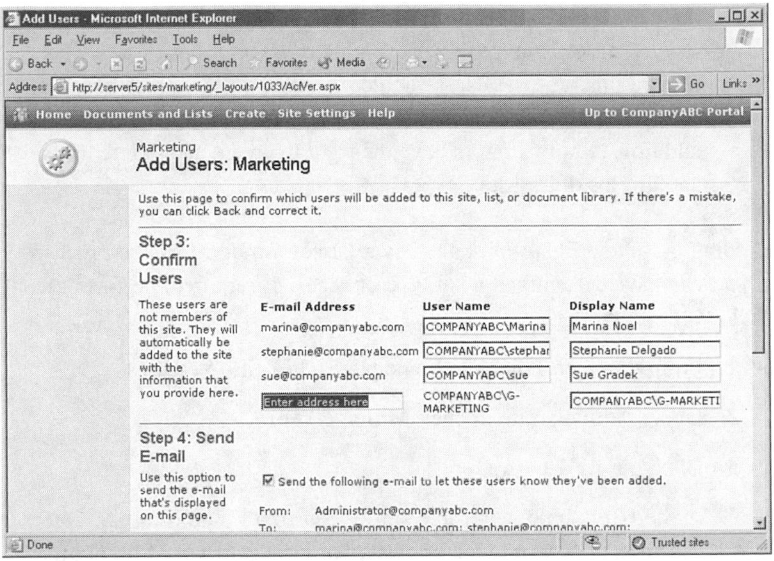

FIGURE 16.1 Adding users to a SharePoint site.

NOTE In the example shown in Figure 16.1, we added an Active Directory group called G-MARKETING into the Contributor site group. Adding groups instead of users is an extremely useful way of setting up sites, because all Active Directory users who are members of that group can then have Contributor access to the site, rather than you having to type in every one of their user accounts.

As a Site Administrator, one of your main jobs will be granting and removing access to a site, so it is important that you understand these concepts and how to manage them.

Creating a Custom Site Group

There may be certain occasions when the default site groups of Reader, Administrator, Web Designer, and Contributor do not provide the level of granularity you require for your site. Fortunately, SharePoint gives you the ability to create your own site group that you can add users to. The site group you create can include any of the following Rights:

- **List rights**
    - Manage List Permissions
    - Manage Lists
    - Cancel Check-Out
    - Add Items
    - Edit Items
    - Delete Items
    - View Items
- **Site rights**
    - Manage Site Groups
    - View Usage Data
    - Create Subsites
    - Manage Web Site
    - Add and Customize Pages
    - Apply Themes and Borders
    - Apply Style Sheets
    - Browse Directories
    - View Pages
- **Personal rights**
    - Manage Personal Views
    - Add/Remove Private Web Parts
    - Update Personal Web Parts
    - Create Cross-Site Groups

To create a custom site group, follow these steps:

1. From the site home page, click **Site Settings**.
2. Under the Administration section, click Go to **Site Administration.**
3. Click Manage Site Groups.
4. Click the **Add a Site Group** link.
5. Type a name for the site group and a description.
6. Enter the rights that members of the site group will have by checking the boxes, as shown in Figure 16.2.

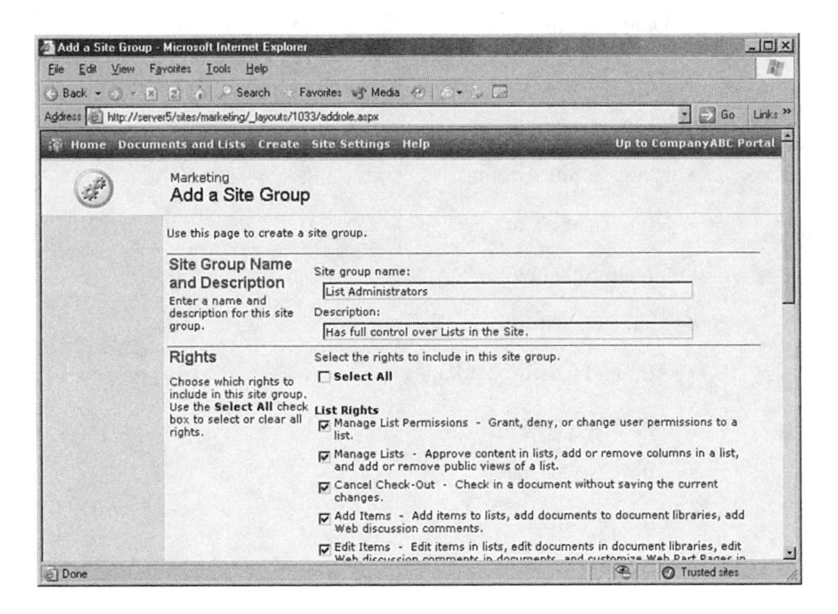

FIGURE 16.2 Creating a custom site group.

7. Click the **Create Site Group** button at the bottom of the page.

Creating your own site groups gives you a much greater degree of flexibility when managing access to your site.

Setting Site Permission Inheritance

If a large number of sites in your SharePoint deployment have the same users, you may benefit from setting up *site permission inheritance*. This allows users from a site "above" the site in question to have access to the subsite. In essence, the permissions and site group memberships "flow down" to the subsites, when sites are configured this way. Site permission inheritance can be configured when a site is first created, or it can be modified at a later time. As a Site Administrator, you can use the following procedure to change permissions to flow down from an above site:

1. From the site home page, click **Site Settings**.
2. Under Administration, click **Go to Site Administration**.
3. Click **Manage Permission Inheritance**. (If you do not see this link, your site is a top-level site, and the option is not valid. This procedure can only be performed on a subsite.)
4. Select **Use the same permissions as the parent site**, as shown in Figure 16.3, and then click **OK**.

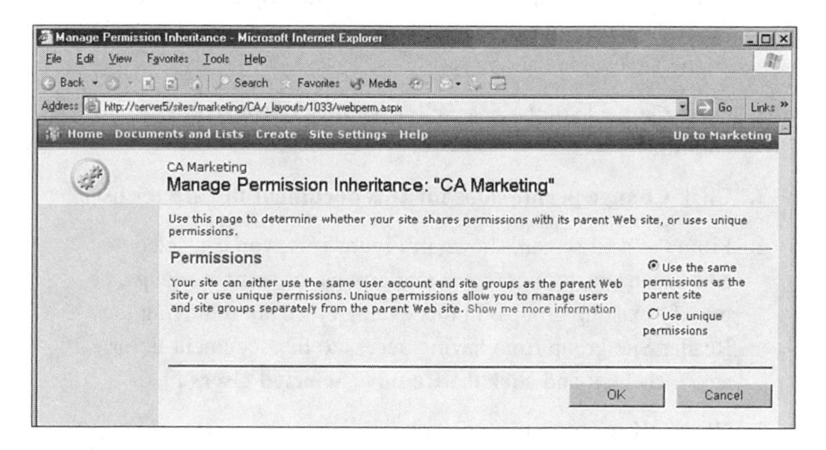

FIGURE 16.3 Changing site permission inheritance.

5. Click **OK** at the warning notice to acknowledge that any customized users or site groups may be lost if you proceed.

Following this procedure and reversing the selection is how you can "detach" a site from a permissions inheritance tree that may be set up. This can be useful if a particular site needs to have a unique set of users.

Configuring List and Library Level Security

After you have added users into the specific site group they need access to, such as Reader or Contributor, those users then inherit those rights across the entire site. If, however, you need to change the ability of certain site groups to access a particular portion of the site, you can modify the security of a particular list or library within your site. This can be useful if you need to give a large group of people Read access to a site, but you also want to restrict them from being able to see information in a specific document library.

To configure specific list or document library security, perform the following steps:

1. Select the particular list or document library by clicking it from the home page of the site or from the **Documents and Lists** link on the navigation bar.
2. On the left side of the page, click **Modify settings and columns**.
3. Click **Change permissions for this document library** (or **list**).
4. From the next screen, shown in Figure 16.4, you can select to add new users, groups, cross-site groups, or domain groups, or modify existing groups. In this example, we are removing the Reader Site group from having access to the document library, so we check it and click the **Remove Selected Users** link.
5. Click **OK** to verify these changes.

Using this procedure, you can get even more granular control over the types of permissions your users require in a site.

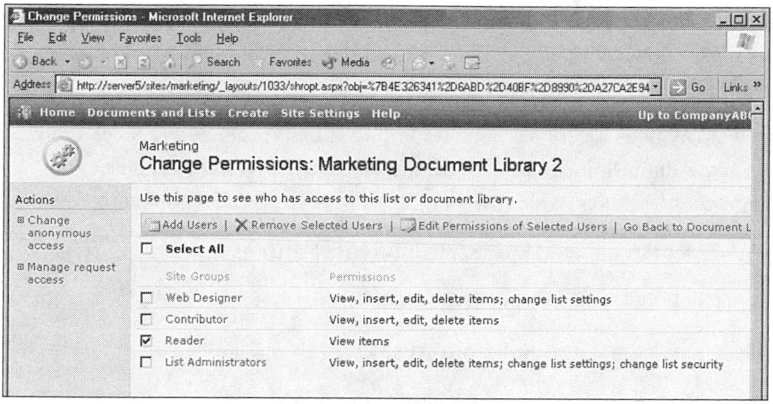

FIGURE 16.4 Modifying document library or list level security.

NOTE One of the questions often asked at this point is whether SharePoint can get even more granular than this with permissions. For example, many Administrators want to be able to delegate permissions at the folder or document level. Unfortunately, this type of functionality is not currently supported in SharePoint, and the only effective way of accomplishing this type of security granularity is to create multiple document libraries or lists and apply security in the manner just discussed.

Managing Anonymous Access to a Site

In certain situations, an organization might want to open a SharePoint site up to anonymous access from the Internet or from other networks. Obviously, some security concerns must be worked through with this, but assuming these concerns have been addressed, two specific tasks must be performed to enable this type of access.

First and foremost, anonymous access must be enabled on a Virtual Server level for the Portal or Windows SharePoint Services site collection. In many cases, you as a Site Administrator may not have access to this, so you may have to send the request up to the Portal Administrator. If you do, you must allow anonymous access from Internet Information Services Manager for the Virtual Server on which SharePoint is installed.

Once anonymous access has been turned on at the Virtual Server level, the various Site Administrators can then decide whether they want to enable anonymous access for their particular site. If you want to set it up, follow these steps:

1. From the site home page, click on **Site Settings**.
2. Click **Go to Site Administration**.
3. Click **Manage Anonymous Access**.
4. On the next screen, shown in Figure 16.5, select what type of access anonymous users should have.

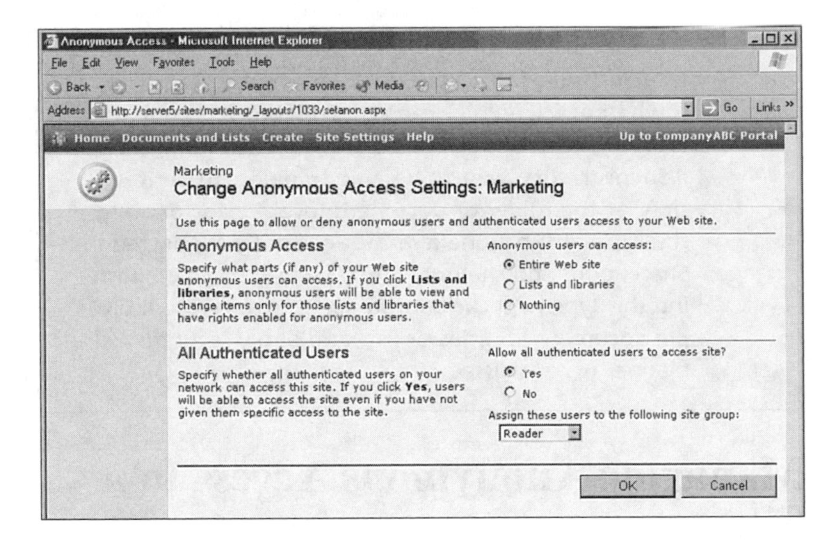

FIGURE 16.5 Allowing anonymous access.

5. Click **OK** to verify these settings.
6. In addition, you can define whether all authenticated users on your network can access the site. This can be useful if you want everyone in your company to be a Reader, for example.
7. Click **OK**.

Anonymous access can make your life easier by removing the need to specifically define all users who can access a site. You should note, however, that great care must be taken when determining whether to turn on this setting, especially if the SharePoint server is exposed to the Internet, because your sensitive information can be easily exposed to snoops and exploits.

Summary

Before anyone can access a SharePoint site, he or she needs to be granted access to that site. A Site Administrator must subsequently understand how to grant users the access they need, without giving them more control than necessary. SharePoint allows you to control this access through the concept of site groups and with the ability to add Active Directory users into a site. Understanding how to administer these concepts is subsequently an important part of being a Site Administrator.

LESSON 17
Home Page Configuration Basics

This lesson demonstrates the main steps involved in adding Web Parts to the home page, changing the views within the Web Parts, and determining which lists and libraries appear in the Quick Launch area.

Exploring a SharePoint Site Home Page

The first thing a user sees when he or she accesses a SharePoint site is the home page. Because first impressions are extremely important, it goes without saying that that home page should contain valuable information and be visually appealing. Fortunately for most of us, SharePoint takes a lot of the grunt work out of creating a useful home page, and it allows most Administrators to create useful and functional home pages without a degree in web design.

Home pages in Windows SharePoint Services vary slightly in look and feel, but they all have essentially the same components. For a review of the components on the page, reference Lesson 1, "Introduction to SharePoint 2003."

Configuring Components on a SharePoint Page

The first step to customizing your page is adding various Web Parts to your zones and modifying them. For example, you may want to add a Web Part that displays the contents of a document library in your site. To do this, perform the following steps:

1. From the home page, click **Modify Shared Page**, select **Add Web Parts**, and click **Browse**.
2. Select a Web Part gallery to use and then select the particular Web Part from the list shown. In this example, select the **Shared Documents** Web Part.
3. You can add the Web Part to the page via two methods. First, you can use the **Add to** drop-down box to select which zone to add the Web Part to and then click **Add**, as shown in Figure 17.1. Second, you can simply drag and drop the Web Part into the appropriate zone.

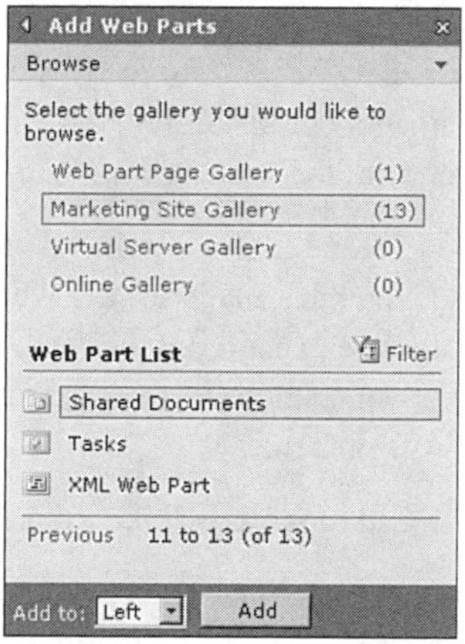

FIGURE 17.1 Adding components to a page.

4. Add additional components to the page as necessary using the same technique. When finished, close the **Add Web Parts** bar by clicking the small X in the upper-right corner of the menu.

Once the Web Part has been added to the page, you can begin customizing the various components to fit your particular needs. For more information on adding and modifying Web Parts, reference Lesson 18, "Adding and Linking Web Parts."

Changing Views on a SharePoint Page

You may not be satisfied with some of the default views that come with the Web Parts you've added to the page. For example, you may want to display only recent announcements or limit the number of documents shown in your document library Web Part. Fortunately, SharePoint is extremely customizable, and you have the ability to modify the views of each Web Part you add to a page. To modify the view of a Web Part, do the following:

1. From the home page of the site, click **Modify Shared Page** and select **Design this Page**.
2. From the Web Part that you want to modify, click the down arrow in the upper-right corner of the Web Part. Choose **Modify Shared Web Part** from the drop-down menu.
3. From the List Views menu that is displayed on the right bar, review the settings you have made for the Web Part by clicking the various plus signs to expand out their corresponding sections. For example, you can modify Appearance, Layout, and Advanced Settings from here.
4. Click the **Edit the Current View** link to modify the view settings.
5. As shown in Figure 17.2, you will be presented with a wide variety of view options for the Web Part view. You can specify which columns to display, how to sort the items, what type of filter to use, item limits, and style. Look through the various available options. Make your changes and then click **OK** when you are finished.

A vast number of view customizations can be performed via this procedure. The following list describes some of the options available to customize the views of the Web Parts:

- **Columns**—The Columns view settings allow you to modify how columns are displayed, giving you the ability to show or hide columns as well as choose in which order they are displayed.

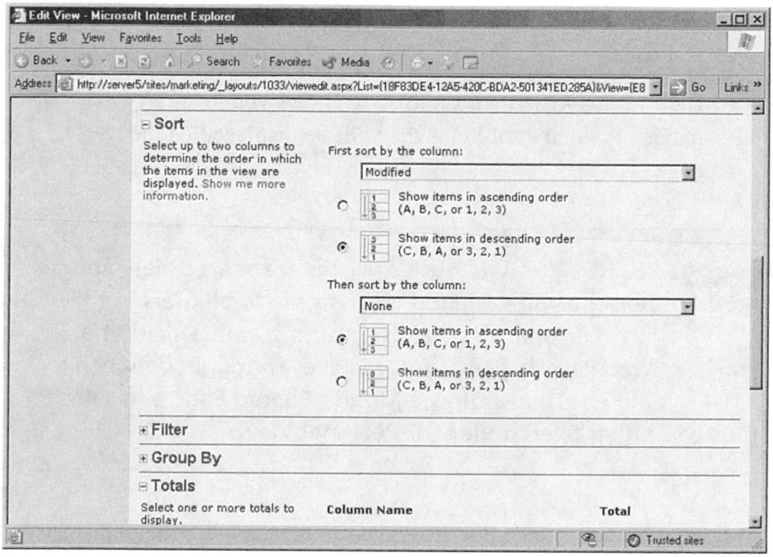

FIGURE 17.2 Editing the view of a Web Part.

- **Sort**—The Sort setting gives you multiple options for sorting the data displayed in the Web Part. This allows you to sort items alphabetically by specific columns.
- **Filter**—The Filter setting allows you to exclude specific pieces of data, depending on criteria you specify. For example, you could choose to only display open items in an issues list.
- **Group By**—Changing the Group By view settings allows you to sort the results by the data entered into specific columns. For example, you could show all "Yes" responses to a survey at the top of the Web Part.
- **Totals**—By modifying the Totals view settings, you can specify whether each column includes a total in the view.
- **Style**—You have multiple Style view settings to choose from, each one displaying information in a different manner. Some of the styles available are Newsletter, Issues Boxed, Shaded, and Basic Table. Each of the views are different, and it is a good idea

to try several out to see which one best displays the information you want to see.

- **Item Limit**—The Item Limit style allows you to specify the maximum number of items that will be displayed on the web page.

NOTE The two types of views are shared view and personal view. Shared views apply to all users in the site. Personal views allow you to create a view of a Web Part that only you can see. To toggle between these settings, choose **Modify Shared Page** and select either **Shared View** or **Personal View**.

Working with views will allow you to customize a web page to display the right information to your users, without displaying too much "busy" information. Displaying the information in an informative way can go a long way toward making the site useful for your end users.

Configuring Quick Launch Settings

The Quick Launch bar on the left side of a SharePoint site can be a useful mechanism for navigating between different pieces of content in a site. For example, if you have multiple document libraries, the Quick Launch bar will give you quick access to those items and allow your users to switch back and forth between them with relative ease.

In certain cases, however, you may want certain site content, such as an announcements list, a survey, or a less commonly used document library, to not show up in the Quick Launch bar. If there are too many items on the bar, its usefulness can be limited.

To configure the individual Quick Launch bar settings for a piece of site content, do the following:

1. From the home page of the site, click **Site Settings** on the Navigation Bar.

2. Under the Customization section, click **Modify site content**.

3. Click the link for the piece of site content you wish to modify. In this example, we will be removing the Shared Documents document library from the Quick Launch bar, so click **Customize "Shared Documents"**.

4. Under the General Settings section, click the link **Change general settings**.

5. On the next page, shown in Figure 17.3, select whether you want the item to appear on the Quick Launch bar. In this example, we are removing it, so we select **No** under the Navigation section.

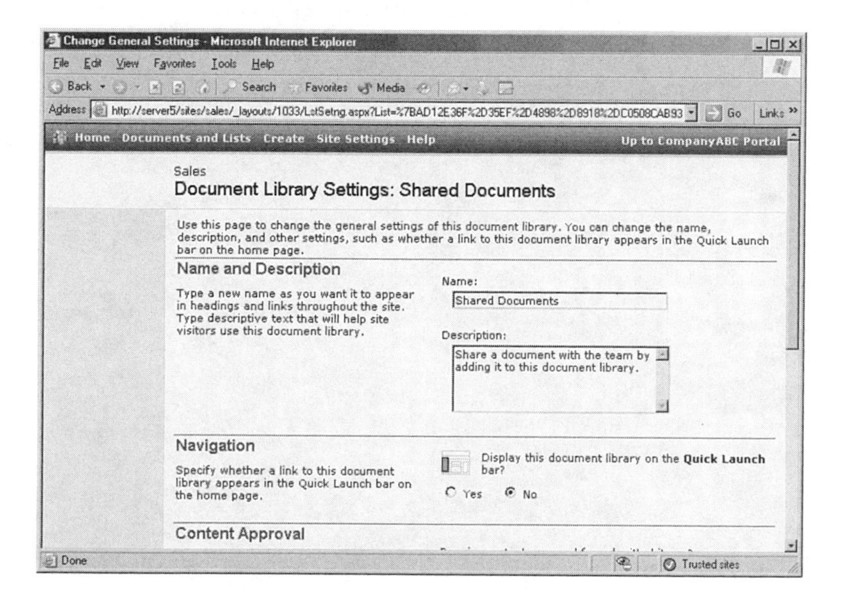

FIGURE 17.3 Editing Quick Launch bar settings.

6. Scroll down to the bottom of the page and click **OK** to save the settings.

From this point, if you click the **Home** link on the navigation bar, you will see that the Shared Documents library is not displayed on the Quick

Launch bar. Finding the right balance of what content to display on this bar can make your site more efficient and well organized.

Summary

As a Site Administrator, it is your job to ensure that your site is displaying the most useful information that will allow your users to do their job in the most efficient manner possible. Fortunately, SharePoint provides for a high degree of customization of its components, and the home page is no exception to this. Customizing what information is displayed in Web Parts, in views, and on the Quick Launch bar can go far toward making your site a success.

LESSON 18

Adding and Linking Web Parts

This lesson gives examples of the basic steps needed to add Web Parts to the SharePoint environment. It covers the process of linking Web Parts on the site home page and demonstrates the use of the Form Web Part.

Understanding Web Parts

A SharePoint site is really just an area that exists solely to house and store information used by its members. That information is presented to the users through logical components added to the site. These components, known as *Web Parts*, display useful information and provide functionality for the users in the site. For example, a Web Part can display the top-10 issues for a project, or simply display the weather forecast.

Web Parts are a critical component for any SharePoint site because they present information in a way that makes it useful. If only raw data was presented on a site, users would be overwhelmed trying to sort through all the available information.

By default, several different types of Web Parts come standard with Windows SharePoint Services:

- **Content Editor Web Part**—This Web Part is used for formatting text, tables and images. This is an extremely useful Web Part because you can cut from documents with rich text, images, and links and paste them into the Web Part. The formatting will stay the same, and no special coding is required.
- **Form Web Part**—This Web Part can be used to create simple HTML forms. The results of the forms can then be input directly

into your Site Content area. You can create the forms in FrontPage or even use straight HTML and just cut and paste the HTML code directly into the Web Part.

- **XML Web Part**—This Web Part is extremely valuable because it can be customized and coded for almost the same type of behavior as a regular web server. Simply by cutting and pasting the HTML or XML code into this Web Part, you can create your own customized Web Part functionality.
- **Document Library/List Web Parts**—These Web Parts are created for each of your document libraries and lists, and they provide for a default view of their contents. Although not the most glamorous, these Web Parts are key to a successful site.

Adding Web Parts to SharePoint Sites

Adding a Web Part to a site is a straightforward task for an Administrator. By default, SharePoint sites are created with a specific number of standard Web Parts that can be dropped into a page. In addition, each piece of site content you create (document libraries, lists, discussions groups) will be represented by a default Web Part. To add one of these Web Parts to a SharePoint site, follow these instructions:

1. From the home page, click the **Modify Shared Page** drop-down link.
2. From the drop-down box, select **Add Web Parts** and then click **Browse**.
3. Select a gallery to choose a Web Part from. For your specific site, it will be named SITENAME Gallery (where SITENAME is the name of your site).
4. As shown in Figure 18.1, select the Web Part you wish to add. You can drag and drop it into the page, or you can select the zone from the **Add to** drop-down box and click the **Add** button. See Lesson 4 “Introduction to Web Parts” for more information on zones.

FIGURE 18.1 Web Parts.

Adding the appropriate Web Parts to a page will make it more informative and useful for your users. In addition, this is the part of the job of Site Administrator that allows you to put on your creative, artistic hat and really design a site that people will use and appreciate.

Importing Web Parts into a SharePoint Gallery

By default, a Windows SharePoint Services site does not contain that many Web Parts in the default Web Part libraries. Fortunately, you can import multiple Web Parts from other sites, portals, or the Internet. Adding Web Parts can be one of the more fun parts of being a Site Administrator, as some of the Web Parts can perform functions and manipulate data in creative ways, such as searching through Active Directory, giving stock updates and news information, and establishing Remote Desktop sessions directly from a SharePoint site.

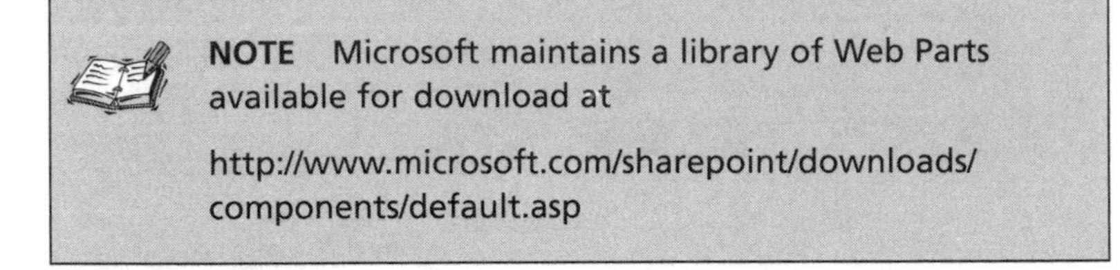

NOTE Microsoft maintains a library of Web Parts available for download at

http://www.microsoft.com/sharepoint/downloads/components/default.asp

To import the DWP file you downloaded into a different site, perform the following steps:

1. Logged in as a Site Administrator, click the **Modify Shared Page** link and navigate to **Add Web Parts** and then to **Import**, as shown in Figure 18.2.

FIGURE 18.2 Importing a Web Part.

2. Click **Browse** to search for the DWP file you exported in previously.

3. Navigate to the DWP file and click **Open**.

4. Click the **Upload** button.

5. The Web Part will now permanently be part of your library for the site. To add it to your page, select a zone for the Web Part from the **Add to** drop-down box and then click **Import**. (You can also drag and drop the Web Part into the zone.)

Once you have a full gallery of Web Parts, you can export those Web Parts to other sites, or you can create a template of the site itself, with all its Web Parts, to be used when creating other sites.

> **NOTE** It is also possible to export Web Parts from a SharePoint Portal Server area to different SharePoint sites. This is a common request among Site Administrators because several Web Parts are only available on a full portal but can be imported into the site via the same process outlined here.

Modifying Web Part Views

Once a Web Part has been added to a page, you can modify its view to display only the information you want users to see on the page. For example, you could modify a Web Part that shows an issues list for a project to only display the top-10 active issues. This type of flexibility gives you control over your Web Parts and what type of information they display. To modify an existing Web Part, follow this procedure:

1. From the page on the site where the Web Part is listed, click the down arrow displayed in the upper-right corner of the Web Part. (For example, if you were modifying the Announcements Web Part, the arrow would be located at the far right of the bar that the word *Announcements* appears on. Choose **Modify Shared Web Part**.

2. At this point, all the options specific to that particular Web Part are listed in a box that appears on the right side of the page. Navigate through those options to get an idea of what is available.

3. In this example, we will change the view for the Web Part. Click **Edit the current view**.

4. The view options will then be displayed, as shown in Figure 18.3. You have many choices. For example, you can filter which items are displayed, which columns are visible, whether there is an icon for the items, and so on. Navigate through each of these choices and select the ones you want. Click **OK** when you are finished.

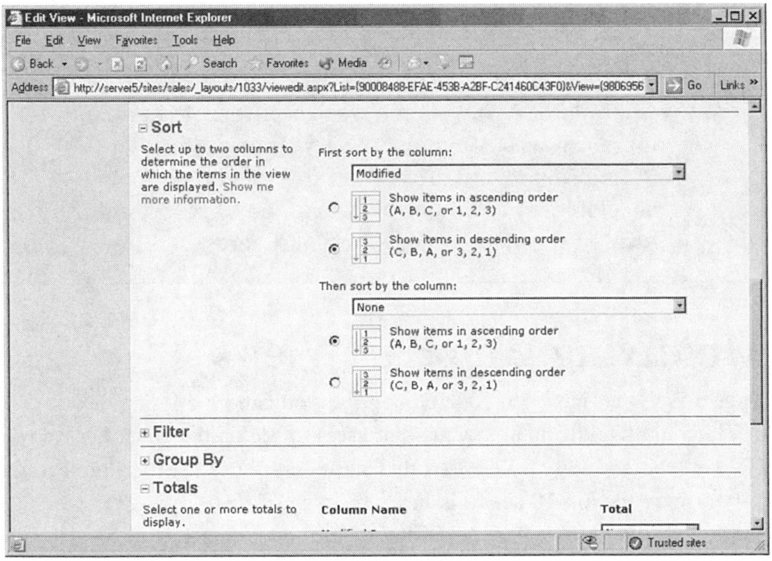

FIGURE 18.3 Modifying a Web Part view.

You have a dizzying array of options to choose from when modifying Web Part views. The benefit to SharePoint lies in the fact that the default "out of the box" functionality gives you a powerful interface, while the control to modify how your data is presented, via the methods described previously, gives you the ability to go beyond the defaults and customize to your heart's content.

Creating Customized XML Web Parts

As previously mentioned, a Web Part is simply a mechanism by which information is displayed. By default, several useful Web Parts are provided, and others can be easily downloaded from the Web and installed. Some administrators, however, may not be satisfied with what is available and may want to create their own Web Parts that display information particular to their site or projects.

Fortunately, you can leverage a built-in mechanism known as an XML Web Part to house customized code to display whatever you can program. You can program your own XML code and input that code directly into the Web Part to make it do what you want. In addition to XML, the Web Part can also use snippets of HTML code, which can be useful if you want to leverage existing code from web pages you've already created or pages from the Internet.

To create and populate an XML Web Part, follow these steps:

1. From the page where you want to add the Web Part, click the **Modify Shared Page** drop-down link.
2. From the drop-down box, select **Add Web Parts** and then click **Browse**.
3. On the Web Part panel that opens up on the right side, choose the appropriate gallery (normally SITENAME Gallery) and choose **XML Web Part** (you may have to click **Next** to view the option).
4. Select the zone to add it to from the **Add to** drop-down box and then click the **Add** button.
5. After the XML Web Part has been added, click the down arrow in the upper-right area of the Web Part and choose **Modify Shared Web Part**.
6. In the XML Web Part options, click **XML Editor** to add your custom code into the Text Entry box.

7. Enter your XML or HTML code into the Text Entry box, similar to what is shown in Figure 18.4. You can cut and paste HTML or XML code from other pages on the Internet with functionality that you want in your Web Part. Click **OK** when you are finished.

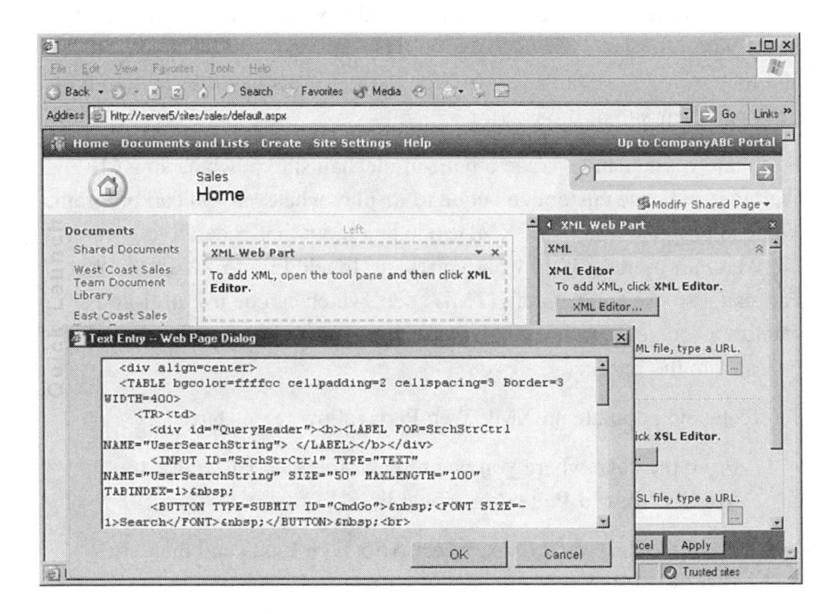

FIGURE 18.4 Populating an XML Web Part with code.

8. Click **OK** again to save the settings.

Summary

Proper placement and use of Web Parts in a site is key to making a particular SharePoint site useful and popular. A SharePoint site can house the most useful documents and list data in the world, but without useful Web Parts to present that data to the users, the site is useless. When it comes down to it, architecting and presenting useful Web Parts on your site is one of the most important things you can do as a Site Administrator to keep your users happy and productive.

LESSON 19
Creating Libraries and Lists

This lesson demonstrates the process of creating a new library or list from the Create menu.

Creating Document Libraries

One of the most common uses for SharePoint products and technologies has been as a document management platform. Indeed, the model that SharePoint uses, where documents are managed, indexed, and modified from within a database, is the model that Microsoft and many other companies are headed for. Central to this concept is the SharePoint document library. A document library is a logical location in a SharePoint site that is used to store documents and other files.

A document library can contain more than just documents. In fact, document libraries can natively support many other different kinds of files, such as Excel spreadsheets, other Office files, Adobe Acrobat files, and even media files. The truth is, you can easily upload any type of file into a document library, although it is most efficient to upload documents and other types of files that can be indexed and searched.

> **NOTE** SharePoint is not a file server replacement location for files such as executables, DLLs, and other system files. In fact, by default, SharePoint will try to block files such as these from being uploaded. You can circumvent these protections, if necessary, but it is important to understand that SharePoint is mainly a document management and portal solution, and not a file server.

Any SharePoint site can contain a number of document libraries. In fact, it is often the case that a particular site will have many document libraries, because the permission structure in SharePoint will not get any more granular than the document library level, which necessitates the creation of multiple document libraries if different permissions are needed.

To create a new document library in Windows SharePoint Services, perform the following steps:

1. From the home page of the site, click the **Create** link on the top bar.
2. Select **Document Library** from the list of options.
3. Enter a name and description for the document library, similar to the one shown in Figure 19.1.

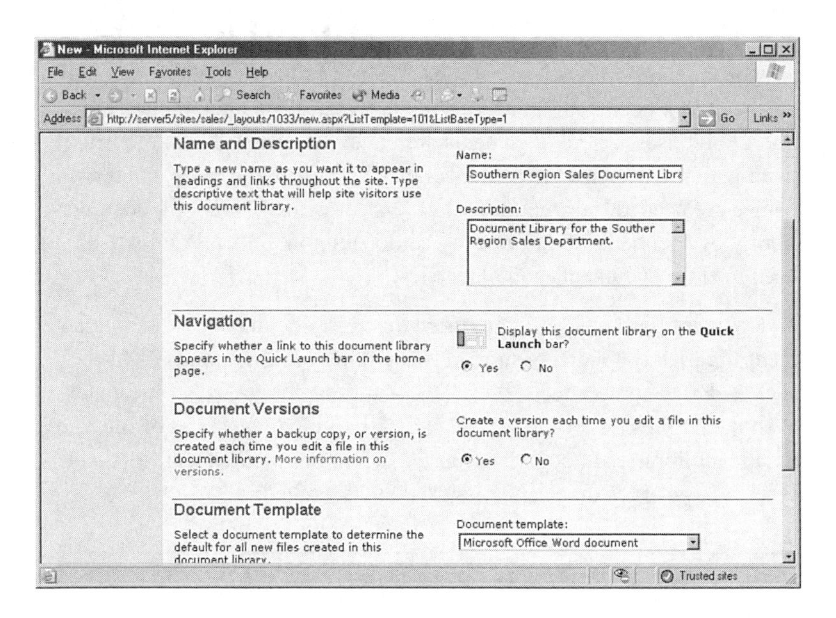

FIGURE 19.1 Creating a document library.

4. Under **Navigation**, select whether to display this document library on the default Quick Launch bar on the left side of the site home page.

5. Under Document Versions, specify whether to create a version each time a file is edited.
6. Under Document Template, choose what the default document template will be when a user creates a new document in this library.
7. Click **Create** when you are finished.

> **NOTE** Once a document library is created, it will not automatically show up on the default view of the site. If you want your users to see it, you will need to place and configure its Web Part on the site. For more information on how to accomplish this, reference Lesson 18, "Adding and Linking Web Parts."

Once created, the document library will exist as part of your site content. You can then add items to the document library or customize the metadata you want associated with the documents.

Modifying Document Library Metadata

After a document library is created, you may want to control the type of metadata that all documents in your library will utilize. For example, you may want to stipulate that all documents contain information on what project they are associated with or whether the documents are confidential. To add in metadata, perform the following tasks:

1. From the SharePoint home page, click **Documents and Lists** from the top bar.
2. Select the document library you wish to modify by clicking it.
3. Select **Modify settings and columns** from the Actions menu on the left.
4. Under the Columns tab, select **Add a new column**.

5. Enter a name for the column. In this example, type in **Project**.

6. Select what type of information this column of metadata will contain. In this example, we want the user to choose from a selection of projects, so we choose **Choice (menu to choose from)**, as shown in Figure 19.2.

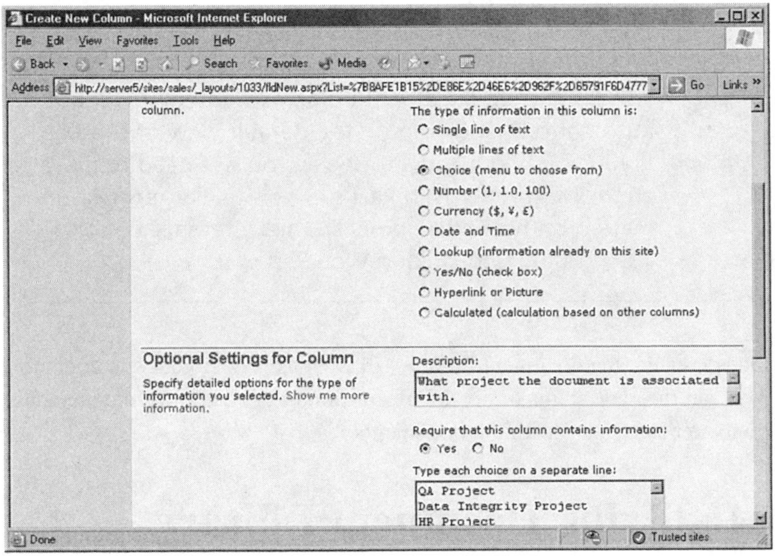

FIGURE 19.2 Adding a metadata column to a document library.

7. Enter a description if necessary.

8. Select whether the metadata column is required by choosing Yes or No under the field **Require that this column contains information**. This can be useful if you want to force users to enter in a value.

9. For the Choice option, you can manually type in each choice in the text box labeled **Type each choice on a separate line:**. In Figure 19.2, you can see that several choices have been added.

10. Choose whether to display the choices using a drop-down menu, radio buttons, or check boxes.

11. Choose whether fill-in choices are allowed and what the default value will be for the field, if any. Fill-in choices allow the user to type in their own values. You can also select whether to add the column of metadata to the default view of the document library.

12. Click **OK** to finish adding the metadata column to the document library.

In this example, every time a document is added to this library, the user will be prompted to enter a project type by choosing from a drop-down box of contents we define. The amount and types of metadata that can be defined are numerous, and they can fit the needs of many document management implementations.

CAUTION When you move documents from one document library to another, the same fields of metadata must exist in both document libraries or else they will be lost.

Creating Standard Lists

Lists are probably the second most useful feature of SharePoint, after document libraries. You can think of lists as really just glorified spreadsheets, with columns and rows of information. What separates SharePoint lists from spreadsheets, however, is the ability for users to collaborate with information in lists in a much more flexible fashion than they would be able to with spreadsheets.

To use a real-world problem as an example, it is common practice for many organizations to email spreadsheets containing timesheets, sales data, parts information, and so on, to members of their team, have them add information to those spreadsheets, and then have them email the spreadsheets back. At that point, some poor intern working in a basement cube has to input all that data back into an isolated database. SharePoint allows the users in the field to automatically enter this information into a simple list, thus saving an enormous amount of time and improving user collaboration. In addition, another benefit of lists is that they allow users to have alerts sent to them whenever information is added or modified.

Although other solutions are available that can perform these types of tasks, the huge advantage that SharePoint provides is that it can do this right out of the box, literally only minutes after you create a site. If you haven't already starting using lists to make your life easier, you should definitely look into it.

SharePoint includes the following default lists as part of a SharePoint site:

- **Links**—A Links list can hold HTML links to web pages and other resources.
- **Announcements**—An Announcements list can be used to inform your site's users of news, special events, and project status and to provide other short clips of information.
- **Contacts**—A Contacts list contains data about members of your team or outside contacts, including phone numbers, email addresses, and other information.
- **Events**—An Events list is used to post date-specific information about appointments, meetings, and the like. Items in an events list can be viewed in calendar format as well, giving your users a good overview of upcoming events.
- **Tasks**—A Tasks lists is used to track the individual items a project or team is working on.
- **Issues**—An Issues list can be used to track a set of problems on a project.

To create a simple list (for example, an Issues list), perform the steps outlined here:

1. From the home page of the site, click the **Create** link on the top bar.
2. Under the Lists section, select the type of list you want to create. For this example, we are creating an Issues list.
3. Type in a name and description and whether you want the list to appear on the Quick Launch bar.

4. Click **Create**. SharePoint will create a list, similar to the one displayed in Figure 19.3.

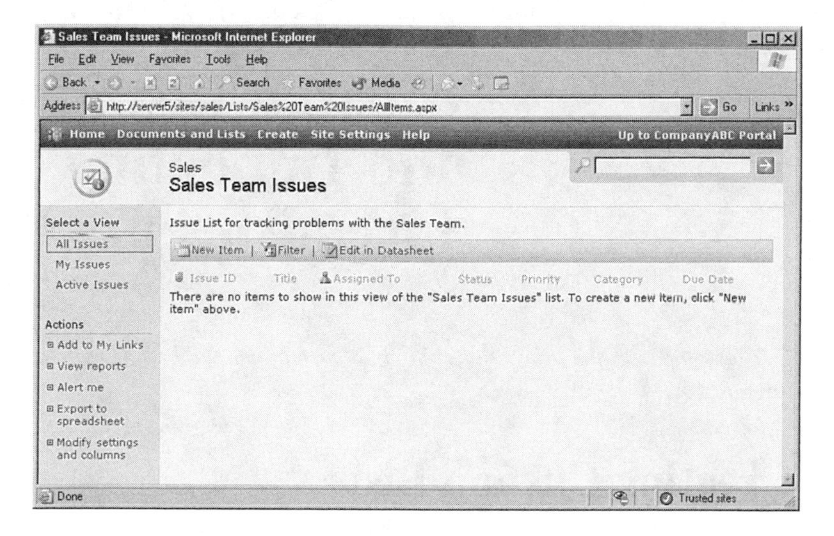

FIGURE 19.3 Creating an Issues list.

Creating the list is only half the battle. To really get full benefit from the list functionality in SharePoint, you have to customize the list to be able to capture and display the type of information you want the list to contain. For more information on this, see Lesson 20, "Creating Custom Lists and Importing Spreadsheets."

Summary

Document libraries and lists are among the most useful components of SharePoint, and they are the mechanisms by which you can really make a site useful. In the real world, these two components are where the vast majority of the activity within a site are accomplished. Understanding how to create and leverage them is consequently a critical step in understanding how SharePoint can make your life easier.

Lesson 20
Creating Custom Lists and Importing Spreadsheets

This lesson covers the process of creating a custom list and importing spreadsheets.

Creating Custom Lists

The list templates provided by SharePoint are extremely useful and cover a wide range of uses. There may be times, however, when the templates provided do not give you all the functionality you require from a list. Luckily, SharePoint makes it extremely straightforward to create custom lists that you can tweak to include data and columns specific to your site. To get started learning how to create custom lists, first create one yourself with the following procedure:

1. From the home page of the site, click **Create** from the top menu bar.
2. Under the Custom Lists section, choose **Custom List**.
3. Enter a name and a description for the custom list. In addition, choose whether you want the list to appear on the Quick Launch bar that shows on the left side of the home page.
4. Click **Create** to finalize the creation of the list.

After the list has been created, you are now ready to proceed forward and modify it by adding custom columns to the list.

Creating and Modifying Columns in a Custom List

Once you have created a custom list, or even if you want to extend some of the default lists SharePoint creates, you can modify it to include the type of information you want the data to contain. For example, you may have a Contacts list that contains phone numbers, addresses, and so on, but you also want it to include a picture of the individuals or maybe even their employee IDs. To add in these extra fields to the data, you need to add "columns" of metadata. SharePoint allows you to create multiple types of columns. For more information on the types of columns, see Lesson 9, "Introduction to Metadata."

To add a column of data to an existing list, follow the procedure outlined here:

1. Navigate to the custom list you just created. To get there, click **Documents and Lists** from the navigation bar and then click the name of the list you created.

2. Click **Modify Settings and Columns** from the action bar on the left.

3. From this page, you can perform several options, such as changing views, adding columns, changing general settings, and changing permissions. In this example, we will be adding columns, so click the **Add a new column** link in the Columns section. In this example, we want to set up multiple regions to associate our data with, so choose the option **Choice (menu to choose from)**, as shown in Figure 20.1.

4. You can also enter a description in the **Description** field.

5. The next radio button is important: It signifies whether the column of data must be entered in for each item in the list or is optional. In this example, choose **Yes** (that it is required).

6. For the **Choice (menu to choose from)** option you chose before, you are now given the option to enter your choices in the next text box, also shown in Figure 20.1. Enter your choices, with each one on a separate line.

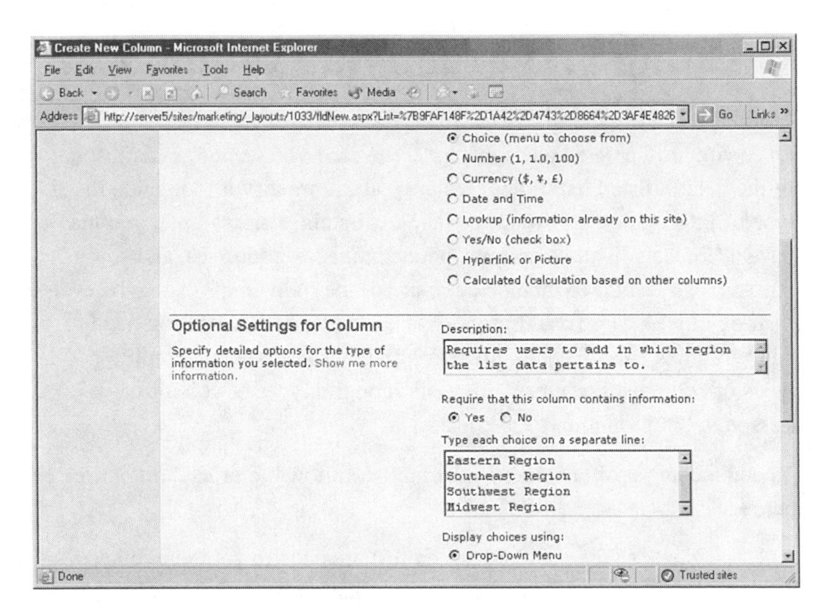

FIGURE 20.1 Entering columns in a custom list.

7. You can choose to display the choices using a drop-down menu (the option used in this example), radio buttons, or check boxes (which allow multiple selections for a response).
8. Finally, fill in the remaining options. You can choose whether to allow "fill-in" choices, what the default will be, and whether to add the column to the default view of the list.
9. Click **OK** when you are finished.

Repeat this procedure as necessary to make sure that you have the right type of data for your list. In addition, you may want to practice adding data to the list to ensure that the columns are being displayed the way you want them and that you are capturing the right type of data for your list.

Creating Custom Lists Using Datasheet View

One of the big improvements in SharePoint 2003 is the ability to have your lists act like real spreadsheets, and to have the flexibility to modify the information in those lists as easily as if you had them open in Excel. To do this, you can create and modify a custom list using Datasheet view.

NOTE To be able to view and modify lists in Datasheet view, you will need a Windows SharePoint Services–compatible spreadsheet program, such as Microsoft Office Excel 2003. Without this software, you will be forced to use the manual methods described in the rest of this lesson.

To create a custom list using Datasheet view, perform the following steps:

1. From the home page of the site, click **Create** on the navigation bar.
2. Under Custom Lists, choose **Create Custom List in Datasheet View**.
3. Enter a name and a description and indicate whether the list will be displayed on the Quick Launch bar.
4. Click **Create** to finalize the creation of the custom list.
5. The list should now open in Datasheet view if you have Excel 2003 installed. It will look similar to the one shown in Figure 20.2, except without data entered in the columns. Make changes to the list like you would in a regular spreadsheet. Any changes you make are automatically reflected in the list.

CAUTION Remember, when working with SharePoint in Datasheet view (and SharePoint in general), there is no "Undo" button, so the changes you make are automatically reflected in the site content!

Any type of bulk changes to a list are made much easier using this technique. Mastering it will greatly simplify your job as a Site Administrator.

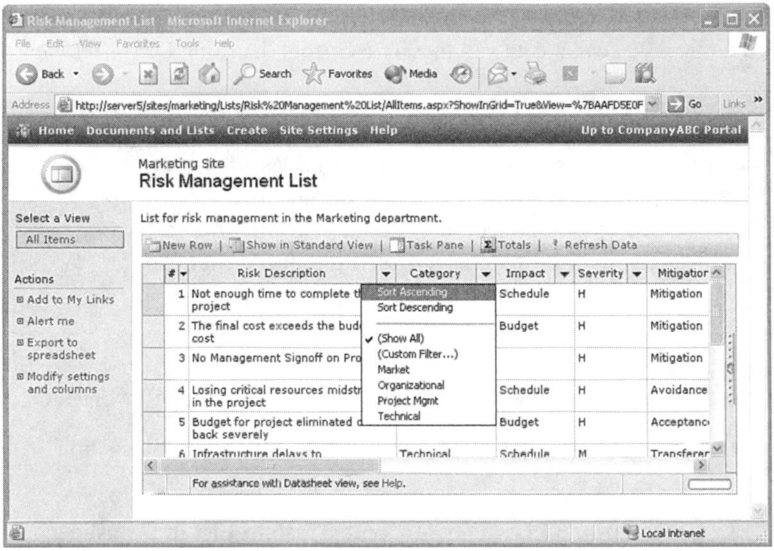

FIGURE 20.2 Creating a custom list in Datasheet view.

Importing Spreadsheets into a List

One of the most common questions about SharePoint is whether existing data can be input into a list easily. Luckily, SharePoint includes the capability to take an existing spreadsheet and automatically input it into a list in a site. The import mechanism automatically creates the necessary columns and rows of data directly from the spreadsheet. This way, you do not have to re-input this information, thus saving yourself a great deal of time.

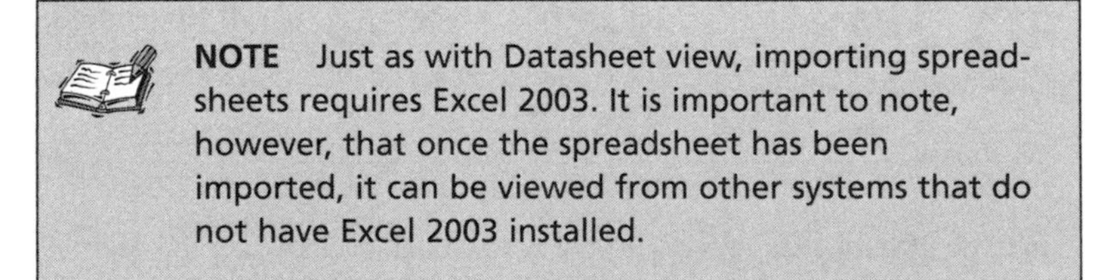

NOTE Just as with Datasheet view, importing spreadsheets requires Excel 2003. It is important to note, however, that once the spreadsheet has been imported, it can be viewed from other systems that do not have Excel 2003 installed.

To import a spreadsheet into a SharePoint list, perform the following steps:

1. From the home page of the site, click the **Create** button on the top bar.
2. In the Custom Lists section, choose **Import Spreadsheet**.
3. Enter a name and a description for the spreadsheet.
4. Under Import from Spreadsheet, enter the file location of the spreadsheet you want to import. You can also click **Browse** to locate the spreadsheet.
5. Click the **Import** button.
6. Excel 2003 will open up, and you'll see a dialog box similar to the one shown in Figure 20.3. You will need to enter the range you want to input. You can do this by choosing **Range of Cells** and typing in the range manually (a whole sheet can be entered by typing in **Sheet1!$1:$65536**, for example). You can also select the **Underscore** button on the right of the Select Range text box and select the cells you want to import.

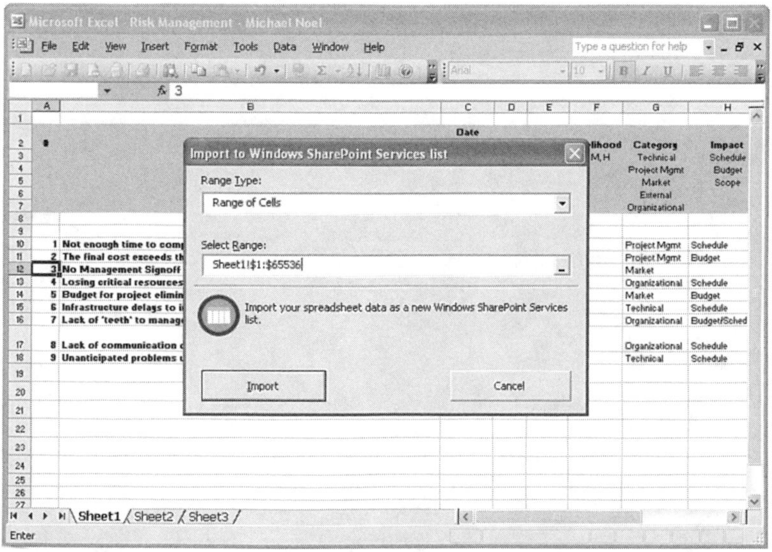

FIGURE 20.3 Importing a Spreadsheet

7. Click **Import** when you are ready.

After the spreadsheet is imported, you may need to go into it in SharePoint and clean it up a bit, because the import mechanism does not always translate the columns the way you might want it to. Using the import technique, however, saves a Site Administrator an incredible amount of data entry time.

Summary

SharePoint lists are an increasingly important part of a SharePoint site. The ability to modify those lists to the needs of your site's users is just as important, and it is subsequently important for you to understand how to create custom lists, modify them, and reduce input time by importing existing spreadsheets of information. With this knowledge, you can greatly improve your efficiency and create a useful and effective site.

LESSON 21
Creating Basic and Web Part Pages

This lesson reviews the processes involved and provides best practice recommendations on creating and using Basic and Web Part Pages.

Creating Basic Pages in a SharePoint Site

SharePoint does not function like a typical web server. Instead of HTML pages, SharePoint utilizes Active Server Pages (.aspx) by default. These types of pages are created in a SharePoint site as Basic and/or Web Part Pages.

Basic Pages and Web Part Pages are pieces of content created and stored in SharePoint document libraries. Although relatively straightforward, this concept takes a while to get used to. Because nearly all SharePoint data is stored in a SQL database, this is the method the SharePoint developers chose for displaying this type of content. So, in a nutshell, if you need to add a simple basic web page to a SharePoint site, you will need to add it to an existing document library and then link to it as necessary.

The first step in understanding how these components work is to create some Basic Pages and Web Part Pages yourself. To create a Basic Page in a SharePoint site, follow the technique outlined here:

1. From the home page of the SharePoint site, click **Create** on the top menu bar.

2. Below the Web Pages section, choose **Basic Page**.

3. Choose a name for the Basic Page and indicate whether you want to overwrite any existing files.
4. Under Save Location, choose which document library you want to add the page to.
5. Click **Create**.
6. A rich-text editor, similar to the one shown in Figure 21.1, will open to allow you to enter in rich text or HTML-formatted content. Enter in what you want and click **Save**.

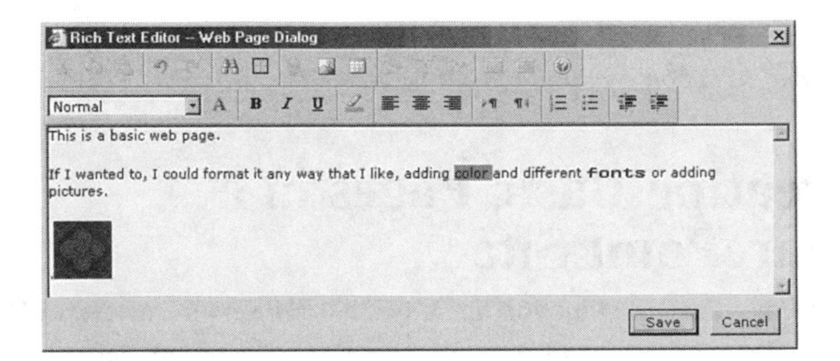

FIGURE 21.1 Using a rich-text editor to create a Basic Web Page.

The page will then be displayed with the formatted text you entered, a top menu bar, and a link for editing the content.

The page itself will be visible in the contents of the document library. You can create a link to the page from anywhere else in the portal, and it will link directly to the page you want. For example, a link to a Basic Page may look something like this:

http://servername/sites/marketing/Shared%20Documents/MarketingPage1.aspx

NOTE It takes a while to get used to the concept of Basic Pages, but once you understand that a document library is similar in concept to a basic folder for holding data, it makes more sense.

Creating Web Part Pages in a SharePoint Site

A Basic Page can be useful, but it's not nearly as functional as a Web Part Page. A Web Part Page can display multiple types of information to your users all at the same time. For example, you can have a stock ticker, a document library, a list of links, a discussion group, and many other sources of content all directed to the end user simply by creating a Web Part Page and adding the respective Web Parts to it.

To create a Web Part Page in Windows SharePoint Services, follow the procedure outlined here:

1. From the home page of the site, select **Create** from the top menu bar.
2. Under the Web Pages section, click **Web Part Page**.
3. Enter a name for the Web Part Page in the **Name** field. This name will use the .aspx extension.
4. Choose a layout template for the Web Part Page, as shown in Figure 21.2. The template you choose will determine how many zones your Web Part Page will have. You'll find more information on the different zone options in the next section of this lesson.
5. Under Save Location, choose which document library to place the Web Part Page in.
6. Click **Create**.

> **CAUTION** Choose wisely when considering what types of zones to add to your Web Part Page. Web browsers with low screen resolutions, such as 1024×768 or lower, may not show all the data in the zones, which may make your site visually unappealing. Be sure to test out different combinations of zones and Web Parts on different client resolutions to find what works best for your site.

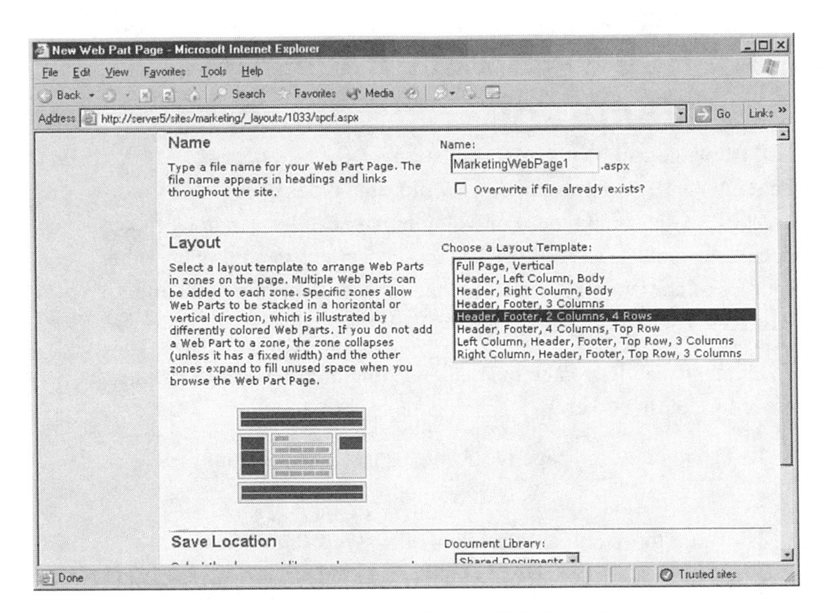

FIGURE 21.2 Choosing a template for a Web Part Page.

The final step in the creation of the Web Part Page is adding the Web Parts to the page. The page will open after it is created, with the zones you chose, as shown in Figure 21.3. Add the Web Parts you feel are necessary. For more information on adding and modifying Web Parts, see Lesson 18, "Adding and Linking Web Parts."

Working with Web Part Page Zones

Each Web Part Page (and the SharePoint site home page, for that matter), contains distinct bounded regions to which you can add Web Parts. These regions are known as *zones*. The zones control how Web Parts are displayed to the end user, and a particular page can contain many zones, as illustrated in Figure 21.3. When creating a Web Part Page or a SharePoint site, you need to understand the differences between the zones, which are detailed in the following list:

- **Full Page zones**—This type of zone covers the entire Web Part Page and is the type of zone you'll want to use if you need your Web Parts to take up all the real estate on the page.

- **Header and Footer zones**—These zones appear at the top and the bottom of the page, respectively. If a great deal of data appears in the middle of the page, the user may have to scroll down to get to the Web Parts in the Footer zone.
- **Column zones**—Column zones are taller than they are wide, and they can be useful for information that looks best when displayed vertically. Normally this type of zone appears on the left and right sides of a page.
- **Row zones**—Row zones are wider than they are tall, and they can be used to hold Web Parts that display information better in this fashion.

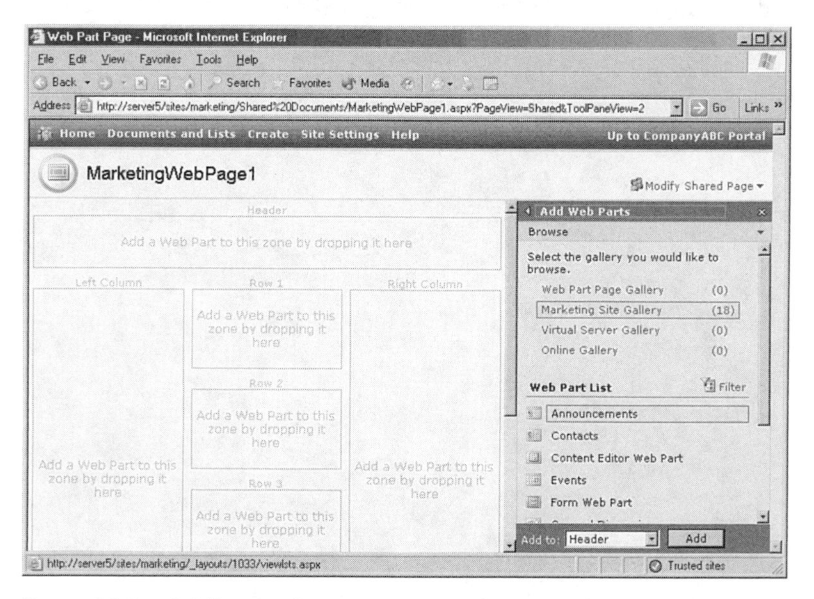

FIGURE 21.3 Adding Web Parts to a newly created Web Part Page.

> **NOTE** Zone width, height, and other criteria can only be modified from a Windows SharePoint Services–compatible editor such as Microsoft Office FrontPage 2003.

It is important to understand how zones work, because they are an integral part in the Web Part Pages you will create in your SharePoint site.

Summary

Basic and Web Part Pages allow you to customize your site's data delivery to your users. You can leverage existing website information by putting it into Basic Pages, or you can customize specific information presented with a Web Part Page. In addition, designing the proper zones for your Web Part Page will help you align the content to display it in a more effective way for your users. Understanding how these types of pages can be created and used is subsequently an important part of being a Site Administrator.

LESSON 22
Forms in SharePoint

This lesson examines the complex topic of effectively creating forms in SharePoint. The uses of a basic list, HTML forms, and InfoPath XML forms are compared and best practice recommendations made.

Understanding SharePoint Forms

Getting information out of your team members' heads and into your SharePoint site is often one of the hardest parts of being a Site Administrator. Fortunately, SharePoint supports several different types of forms, the information from which can be input directly into SharePoint lists.

A nearly unlimited supply of various types of forms can be created in SharePoint. You can set up Human Resources forms such as vacation request forms or timesheet forms. You can create customized forms using an XML form creator such as Microsoft Office InfoPath 2003. Finally, you can create "old-fashioned" HTML forms, using a program such as Microsoft Office FrontPage 2003, and have those forms embedded in your SharePoint site. Finding the right combination of forms to perform the job can do wonders in improving your overall site's efficiency.

Creating HTML Form Web Parts for SharePoint

The most basic type of form that can be utilized in SharePoint is the traditional HTML-based form. This type of form has been used on HTML pages on traditional websites for years, and it's not difficult to create. Many different types of programs exist for creating HTML forms, and all you need for importing these forms into SharePoint is the actual code of the forms themselves. For example, if you are using FrontPage, you can simply run the Form Wizard to create a form and then copy and past the code information into a Form Web Part in SharePoint.

> **NOTE** The HTML Form Web Part is only useful if you have existing HTML forms that you want to transfer to a SharePoint site. The procedure outlined here describes how to create this Web Part, with the assumption that you will be copying and pasting HTML code from an existing form, or one that you created using an HTML Editor such as FrontPage.

To create and populate a Form Web Part in SharePoint, do the following:

1. From the page where you want the Web Part Page to appear, click the **Modify Shared Page** link in the upper-right corner of the site.
2. Navigate to **Add Web Parts** and then click **Browse**.
3. From the default Web Part gallery, click **Form Web Part**.
4. From the **Add to** drop-down box, choose a zone to add the Web Part to and then click **Add**. You can also perform this step by dragging and dropping the Web Part into the appropriate zone.
5. Close the **Add Web Part** box by clicking the X in the upper-right corner of the dialog box.
6. Click the down arrow in the upper-right corner of the Form Web Part on your page and choose **Modify Shared Web Part**.
7. Click the **Source Editor** button to open the HTML Source Code dialog box.
8. Paste HTML code into the text entry box, as shown in Figure 22.1. You can use any HTML-formatted forms, such as those created with Microsoft FrontPage for the Web Part.
9. Click **Save** and then click **OK** to close the Form Web Part dialog box.

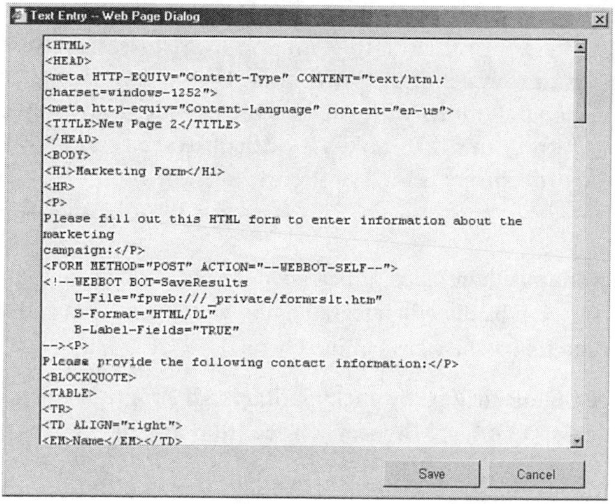

Text Entry -- Web Page Dialog

```
<HTML>
<HEAD>
<meta HTTP-EQUIV="Content-Type" CONTENT="text/html;
charset=windows-1252">
<meta http-equiv="Content-Language" content="en-us">
<TITLE>New Page 2</TITLE>
</HEAD>
<BODY>
<H1>Marketing Form</H1>
<HR>
<P>
Please fill out this HTML form to enter information about the
marketing
campaign:</P>
<FORM METHOD="POST" ACTION="--WEBBOT-SELF--">
<!--WEBBOT BOT=SaveResults
    U-File="fpweb:///_private/formrslt.htm"
    S-Format="HTML/DL"
    B-Label-Fields="TRUE"
--><P>
Please provide the following contact information:</P>
<BLOCKQUOTE>
<TABLE>
<TR>
<TD ALIGN="right">
<EM>Name</EM></TD>
```

Save Cancel

FIGURE 22.1 Entering an HTML form into a SharePoint Form Web Part.

You can use these types of forms to leverage existing forms you've created in the past or to support clients without XML-compatible editors such as InfoPath that can't take advantage of the more SharePoint-integrated XML forms.

Creating XML Forms in InfoPath

The most functional type of forms in SharePoint are XML forms, which are created using the recently popular Extensible Markup Language (XML). XML forms are extremely functional and can be tied in directly to SharePoint so that the results of the forms are directly entered into a list in the site.

There is a catch, however. To be able to fill out these forms, your users need to utilize a Windows SharePoint Services–compatible XML viewer such as Microsoft Office InfoPath 2003. InfoPath makes creating and customizing forms a piece of cake, and it is recommended that you install InfoPath just to try out this functionality.

> **NOTE** Unfortunately, in modern IT infrastructures it is rare to run into environments that have fully deployed InfoPath. Although this may change in the future, this fact makes it difficult to roll out ambitious forms projects in SharePoint.

If you have InfoPath installed, it is a good idea to build some forms and test how they can be directly integrated into your SharePoint site. To do this, you can follow the steps outlined here:

1. Open InfoPath 2003 by clicking **Start**, **All Programs**, **Microsoft Office**, **Microsoft Office InfoPath 2003**.
2. On the **Fill out a form** bar on the right side of InfoPath, choose **Design a Form**.
3. From the **Design a new form** section, choose **Customize a Sample**.
4. Choose a form to test from the list of sample forms shown in Figure 22.2. Click **OK**.

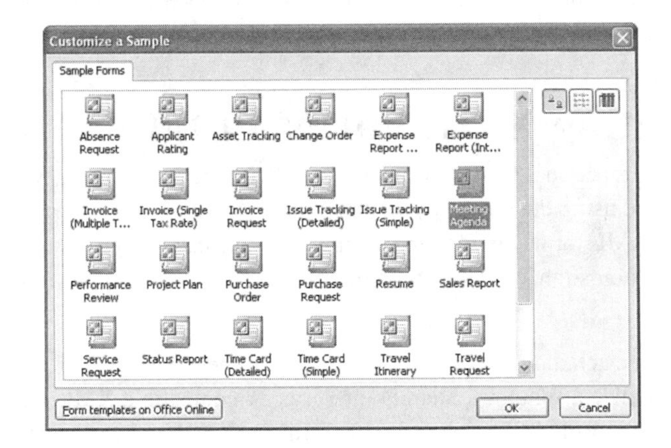

FIGURE 22.2 Choosing a sample InfoPath form.

5. When the sample form opens in InfoPath, play around with some of the available options. InfoPath offers rich options for various forms that can be built. When you are finished making customizations, choose **File, Save**.

6. Click **Publish** to save the form into SharePoint.

7. When the Publishing Wizard is displayed, click **Next** to continue.

8. On the next screen, shown in Figure 22.3, choose to publish the form to a SharePoint form library by selecting the second option and clicking **Next**.

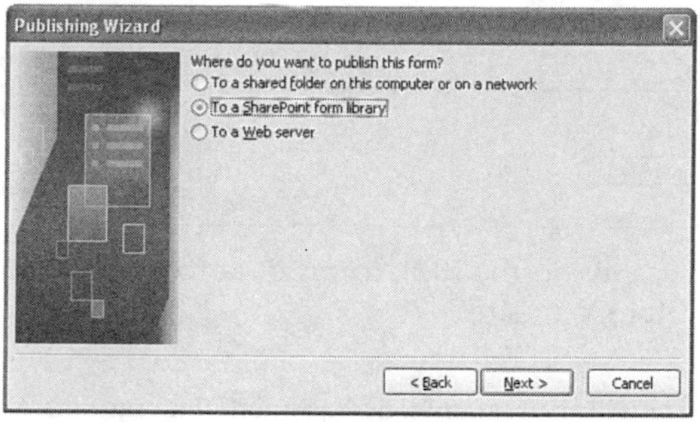

FIGURE 22.3 Publishing an InfoPath XML form to a SharePoint form library.

9. Choose **Create a new form library (recommended)** and click **Next**.

10. Enter the HTTP location of the site you want to add the form to (for example, http://servername/sites/marketing) and click **Next**.

11. Authenticate if prompted.

12. Type in a name and a description for the form library. Click **Next**.

13. The next screen, shown in Figure 22.4, is critical to capturing the right type of data into SharePoint. Choose the fields from the form that you want entered into SharePoint columns. These fields will be entered in as a list and can be utilized for many different purposes in your SharePoint site. Click the **Add**, **Remove**, and **Modify** buttons to add in the proper columns. Click **Finish** when you are finished.

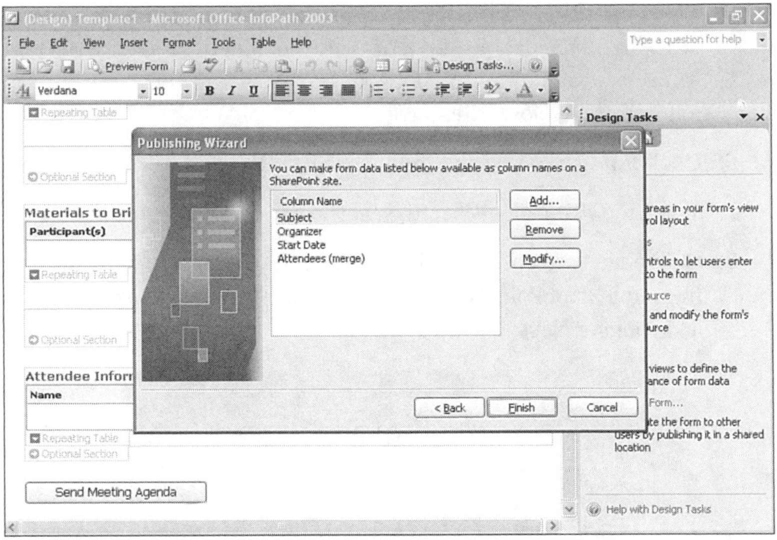

FIGURE 22.4 Choosing the XML forms data to use for column names in a SharePoint site.

14. The form will then be uploaded as a template into the XML forms library you created. At the final screen, select whether to notify users and then click **Close** to finish the process.

Anyone who accesses the forms library you just created will be able to fill out the form and have the information inputted directly to the site.

Filling Out Forms in a SharePoint XML Forms Library

Once a form has been used to create a SharePoint XML forms library, that form has to be filled out to be useful to you. For example, you can have an XML form template that users fill out for their timesheets each week. All the timesheet data is then stored in the XML forms library and can be reported on and monitored as necessary.

The reality is that many types of XML forms libraries can be created, and it doesn't take much to get this type of functionality in place. To fill out an XML form using the InfoPath client, follow these steps:

1. From the site home page, click **Documents and Lists** from the top menu bar.
2. Under Document Libraries, choose the name of the XML forms library you created in the previous section.
3. Click the **Fill Out This Form** button in the XML forms library.
4. After InfoPath opens, fill out the form data. Depending on the form you chose to create as the template, this step will vary. After you are done filling out the form, choose **File**, **Save from InfoPath**.
5. Choose a name for the form and save it into the site by clicking the **Save** button.

Once you have entered in the data into the form, it will show up in the forms library as columns, similar to Figure 22.5. As you can see, this can be a very powerful tool for obtaining information from the members of your team.

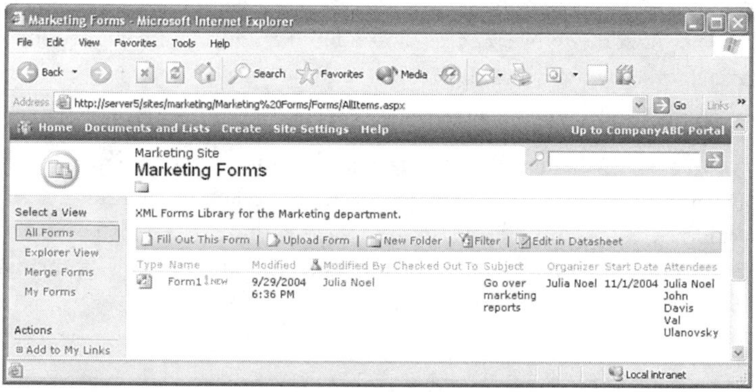

FIGURE 22.5 Filling out an XML form.

Summary

Forms are an extremely useful feature in SharePoint 2003. Integrating SharePoint with the use of an XML client such as InfoPath 2003 can further extend the functionality of both environments. Giving your users options, such as those provided with forms, can help you consolidate your information into a centralized location and increase the usefulness of your SharePoint site.

Lesson 23
Creating Sites

This lesson reviews the templates provided and discusses the process of creating new sites and workspaces, using both the default templates and your own customized templates.

Understanding the Site-Creation Process

Sites in Windows SharePoint Services are the centerpiece of activity within SharePoint. All data is managed and controlled from within the confines of separate sites, and each site is made to be self-sufficient. In fact, sites can be thought of as "islands" of data, each independent from each other in content, user access, and administration, but designed to tie into each other when necessary.

As a Site Administrator, it is often necessary for you to create new sites for your users—whether for a separate project or a separate department or group of users within your organization. Because nearly all other activity in Windows SharePoint Services takes place within a site, it is greatly important that you understand how to create new sites and how to manage the sites you create.

Understanding Sites and Workspaces

In addition to the concept of a SharePoint site, Windows SharePoint Services includes the concept of a *workspace*. A workspace is a subsite designed for managing information concerning meetings, events, and other tasks that are part of the functions of an existing site. For example, you may have a SharePoint site for the IT department, but create a Meeting workspace to manage meetings about a specific IT upgrade project.

Both sites and workspaces take up the same logical space, and both can include separate sets of user accounts, if necessary. For example, a top-level site (for example, http://servername/sites/marketing) may contain a subsite (for example, http://servername/sites/marketing/bobsgroup) and a workspace (for example, http://servername/sites/marketing/clientmeetings). In this respect, the sites and workspaces take the same space in the logical SharePoint hierarchy.

The concept of a workspace is similar to that of a site, with the exception that workspaces in SharePoint look and act slightly different from sites. Figure 23.1 shows a sample Social Event workspace, which can be used to organize a social meeting. On each workspace, as you'll notice, the Quick Launch bar is not displayed and the content is managed through the Modify This Workspace link on the right of the page. In addition, the user navigates the content in the workspace through the use of "pages" that show up as tabs on the site. This format, although different, is efficient in its own way, and SharePoint workspaces can become effective tools for managing "side projects" or activities that fall under the auspices of a standard SharePoint site but require their own functional area.

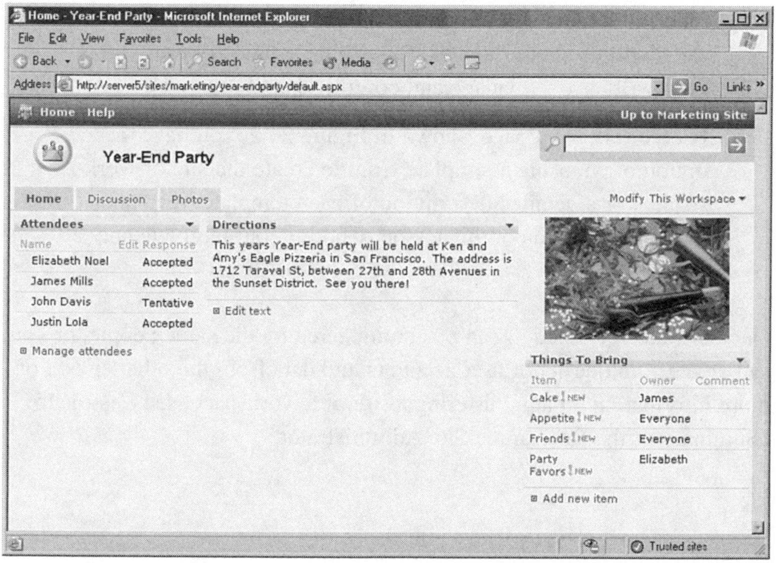

FIGURE 23.1 Examining a workspace.

Creating Sites and Workspaces

In many cases, throwing all your users into a single site and expecting them to get everything done in that one site is not efficient. It often helps to break down the tasks your organization performs into multiple component, and then create multiple SharePoint sites or workspaces for those specific functions. For example, you could create a SharePoint site for each of the departments in your organization, or you could have an individual site for each project.

To create a new site or workspace in an existing SharePoint site, follow the procedure outlined in the following steps:

1. From the home SharePoint site (the parent site), click **Create** from the top menu bar.
2. Select **Sites and Workspaces** from the Web Pages section.
3. Enter a title and description for the site.
4. Enter the URL address where this site will reside.
5. From the Permissions section, select whether this site will inherit the same permissions as the parent site (the same set of users will use both sites) or if it will have unique permissions (you will have to manage and control separate sets of users).
6. On the following page, shown in Figure 23.2, you have the option of choosing a template from to create the site or workspace. For a detailed description of each template, read ahead to the next section of this lesson. Choose your template and click **OK**.

Once the site is created, it can be administered by the same people, or you can create a unique set of user accounts and data from the other sites. For more information on administering a site or a workspace, see Lesson 15, "Summary of the Role of the Site Administrator."

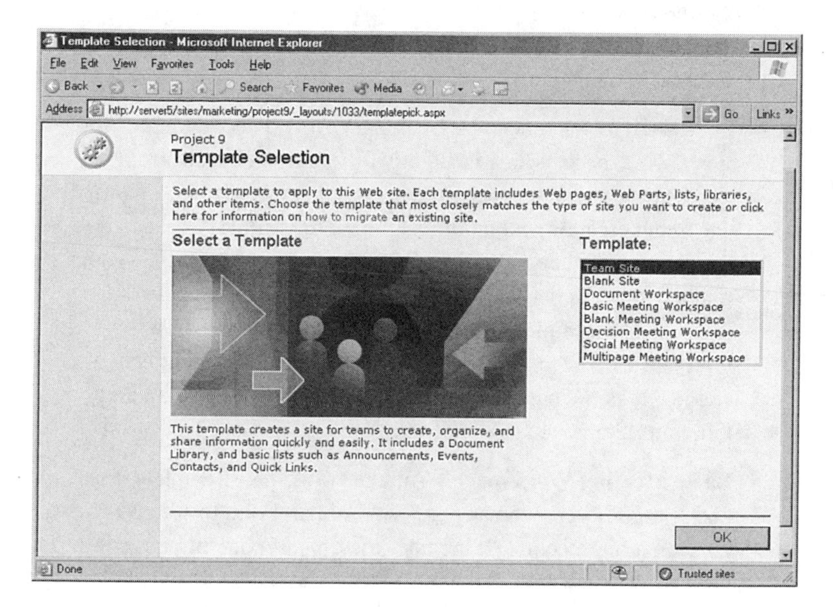

FIGURE 23.2 Creating a new site.

Understanding Default Site Templates

Right out of the box, Windows SharePoint Services includes common site templates that can be used to create new sites. These templates include the most commonly requested site functionality for SharePoint and can be further customized after their creation. The types of site templates included in SharePoint are as follows:

- **Team Site**—The Team Site template is one of the most common templates used to create sites. This template includes standard site items such as a shared documents library and Announcements, Event, Contacts, and Quick Links lists. The template creates a site with two zones for Web Parts—a larger left zone and a smaller right zone.

- **Blank Site**—The Blank Site template creates the same site structure as the Team Site template, but without the default content such as document libraries and lists. You can easily add your own content after the site is created. The zones created are the same as in the Team Site template.

- **Document Workspace**—A Document Workspace template creates a workspace, which is slightly different in concept from a site. This template creates a workspace that can be used when document creation and modification are the primary reasons for the creation of the workspace. It includes a document library and Links and Tasks lists for managing the document-creation process. This template is normally used by members of a top-level site who need a space to focus solely on document creation. The home page for the site includes three zones—a top, left, and right zone.
- **Basic Meeting Workspace**—Another workspace template, this one is used if you need a space within SharePoint to set up and manage a big meeting. It includes the type of content you would need to organize and track your meeting, such as Objectives, Attendees, Agenda lists, and a document library. This workspace looks and feels different from a regular site—it doesn't have a Quick Launch bar or a full top link bar, and it changes the way common tasks are done. For example, content is created and controlled through pages in the workspace. These pages can be created to display separate sets of content from the workspace using tabs. Zones are split into three columns—left, right, and center.
- **Blank Meeting Workspace**—A Blank Meeting workspace is simply the Basic Meeting workspace, but without the predefined content. Administration is different than with a regular site because all actions are controlled from the link on the right of the workspace labeled **Modify This Workspace**. Use this tool to define user settings, create content, and manage page layout.
- **Decision Meeting Workspace**—A Decision Meeting workspace is essentially the same as the other meeting workspace templates, except that a few extra lists are created. The template includes a predefined document library and lists for objectives, attendees, agenda, tasks, and decisions. Zones are also split into three columns.

- **Social Meeting Workspace**—This type of workspace is useful when you are setting up an event or a social occasion for your site users. The workspace includes a default picture library for posting pictures of the event, as well as several lists, such as Attendees, Directions, Things to Bring, and Discussions. Zones are split into three columns, as with the other workspaces.
- **Multipage Meeting Workspace**—This workspace includes multiple pages that you can define based on the needs of your project. By default, it also includes Objectives, Attendees, and Agenda lists. The three column zones are present on this workspace as well.

During the site-creation process discussed previously, you had the option to choose one of these templates to use when creating your site. Because SharePoint is easily customizable, you'll find it straightforward enough to customize you site even further after it is created.

Creating and Using Customized Site Templates

If you are not satisfied with the functionality of the default site templates or you want to create a large number of "branded" sites with company logos, default content, and the like, you do have the option of creating and customizing your own site template that can be used in the creation of future sites. Once you set it up, the template will show up as an option when you create any new site, making it easy for you to easily create multiple sites with the exact content you desire.

To set up a customized site template, you must first export an existing site to a Site Template file (.stp). To do this, follow these steps:

1. From the site home page, click **Site Settings** from the top menu bar.
2. Under the Administration section, click **Go to Site Administration**.
3. Under the Management and Statistics section, click **Save site as template**.

4. Enter a filename for the template along with a title, such as the one shown in Figure 23.3.

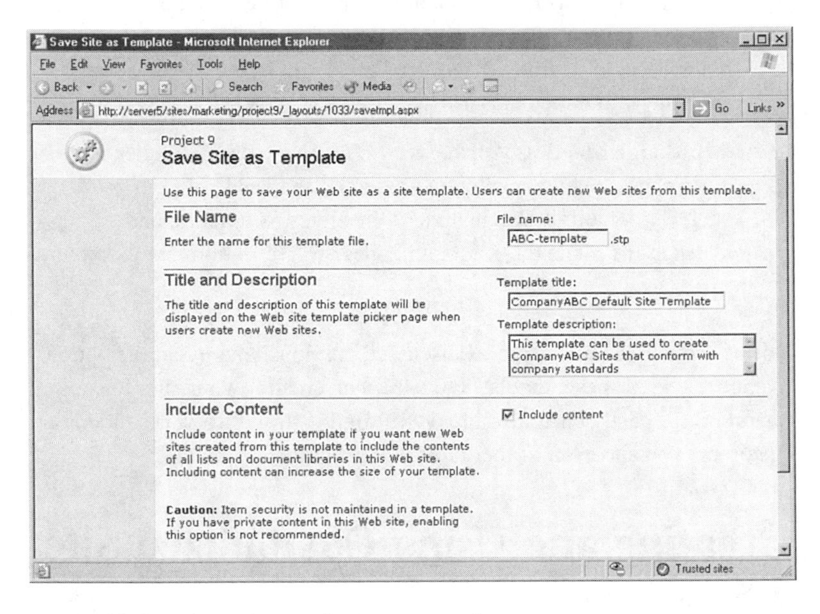

FIGURE 23.3 Exporting a site to a template.

5. Under Include Content, select whether you want the content in the site to be a part of the template. For example, you may want the content of document libraries, lists, and the like to be exported to the template.

6. Click **OK** to export.

CAUTION There is a hard limit of 10MB to the size of a Site Template file, so be sure not to attempt to export too much data from a site to a template; otherwise, the process will fail.

Once your template is added into the default Site Template gallery, you will be able to choose it from the list of templates when you create new sites in SharePoint. You can add multiple templates to this gallery as needed; this is often a very useful way to streamline the creation of sites and workspaces.

Summary

Sites and workspaces are essentially the key components of SharePoint where all activity takes place. Projects, teams, departments, and other units can function best within SharePoint if they are given their own space to work in, with their own set of content. Subsequently, a critical part of being a Site Administrator involves matching the layout of sites and workspaces in SharePoint to your organizational structure.

LESSON 24
Backup Strategies

This lesson discusses methods for backing up sites and lists by creating a template and saving the contents and by using FrontPage 2003 to back up and export sites.

Understanding the Backup Process in SharePoint

Nothing is worse than having a successful SharePoint site lost to a hard drive crash or corruption. Although often overlooked, backing up and restoring your SharePoint data is a crucial component to any SharePoint implementation.

Although Enterprise tools are available for backups in products such as SharePoint Portal Server 2003, Windows SharePoint Services sites are slightly different in their approach to backups. Fortunately, some easy-to-use tools and processes can be deployed to back up SharePoint sites on a regular basis. Understanding how to use these tools and processes is key.

TIP A permanent backup solution using a vendor such as Veritas should be considered for any production SharePoint implementation.

Backing Up SharePoint Sites Using FrontPage 2003

One simple solution to backing up a SharePoint site is to use FrontPage 2003. Because a SharePoint site is essentially a compilation of web pages and other web-specific information, it can be easily backed up from a utility such as FrontPage.

CAUTION Only the 2003 version of FrontPage supports backups in SharePoint 2003 (it's the only version that even works with SharePoint 2003). Therefore, it is important to run the proper version before connecting to your WSS site.

To perform a backup of a SharePoint site using FrontPage, perform the following steps:

1. Open Microsoft Office FrontPage 2003.
2. Go to **File**, **Open Site**.
3. In the **Site name** field, enter in the URL of the site you want to back up (for example, http://servername/sites/marketing) and then click **Open**.
4. Authenticate if prompted.
5. Go to **Tools**, **Server**, **Backup Web Site**.
6. When prompted with the dialog box in Figure 24.1, check the box labeled **Include subsites in archive** (if you want to back up all site and subsites) and then click **OK**.
7. Enter a name and a location for the backup file (.fwp) that will be created and then click **Save**.
8. The backup procedure will begin and a progress bar similar to the one shown in Figure 24.2 will be displayed. After the backup is finished, you can click **OK**.

This technique is useful because you can run it from an Administrator's desktop in the middle of the day or any time you make substantial changes to a site.

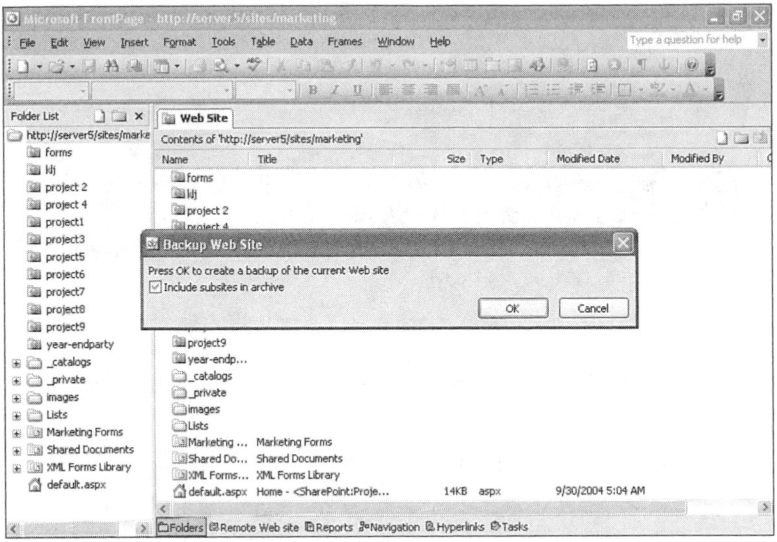

FIGURE 24.1 Backing up the SharePoint site with FrontPage.

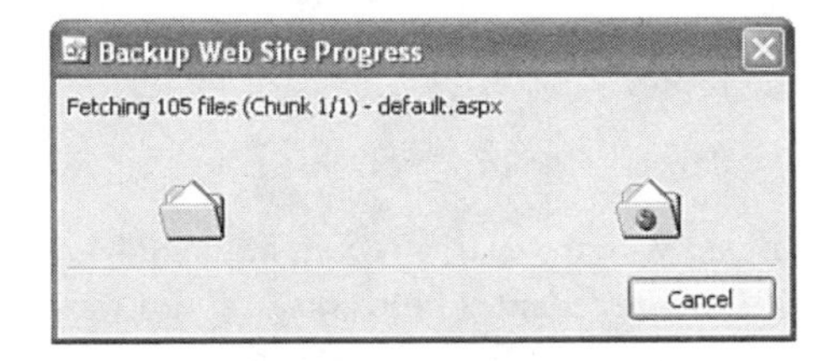

FIGURE 24.2 FrontPage backing up the SharePoint site.

> **CAUTION** Although the FrontPage approach restores most site content, it often does *not* restore security settings in the same way. You may have to restore some of the security on document libraries and lists after you run the restore. If you desire to restore all aspects of a site, you will need to use an Enterprise tool such as Veritas or a utility such as STSADM.EXE, which is included on a SharePoint server and is described in more detail in Chapter 25, "Migrating and Moving Data."

Deleting and Re-creating Sites in Anticipation of a Full Restore

If you need to restore a site you backed up, you will first need to ensure that the old site does not exist. In some cases, when you're rebuilding a server, the site will not exist, but in other cases, such as the site becoming corrupt or losing data, you will need to delete the site first.

> **CAUTION** Do not perform a deletion of your site unless you actually need to restore it from a backup or if you are performing the operation on a test site or server. In addition, you will need to have full Site Administrator rights to perform this operation.

To delete a site in anticipation of restoring it from backup, perform the following steps:

1. From the site home page, click **Site Settings** on the top link bar.
2. Under Administration, click **Go to Site Administration**.
3. Under Management and Statistics, choose **Delete this site**.
4. When presented with the screen in Figure 24.3, click **Delete**.
5. You will be prompted that your site was deleted once the process has completed.

After you have deleted the site, you must re-create it in Windows SharePoint Services in the same location it was previously. The only exception to the standard site-creation process is that you should not apply a template when creating the site. To illustrate, when you get to the screen shown in Figure 24.4, do not proceed any further and simply navigate away from the page. If you apply the template, the restore will fail, with a message stating that you can't restore to a site that already has a template applied. You will have to delete the site again and re-create it as a blank site if this happens.

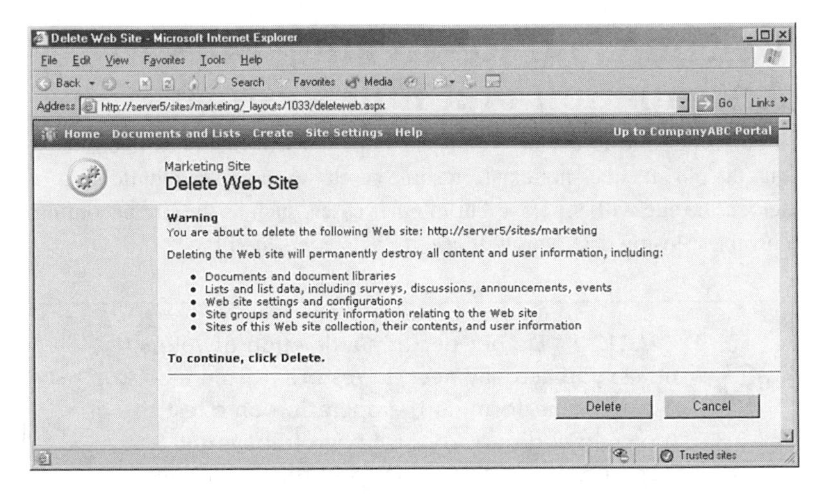

FIGURE 24.3 Deleting a SharePoint site so that it can be restored later.

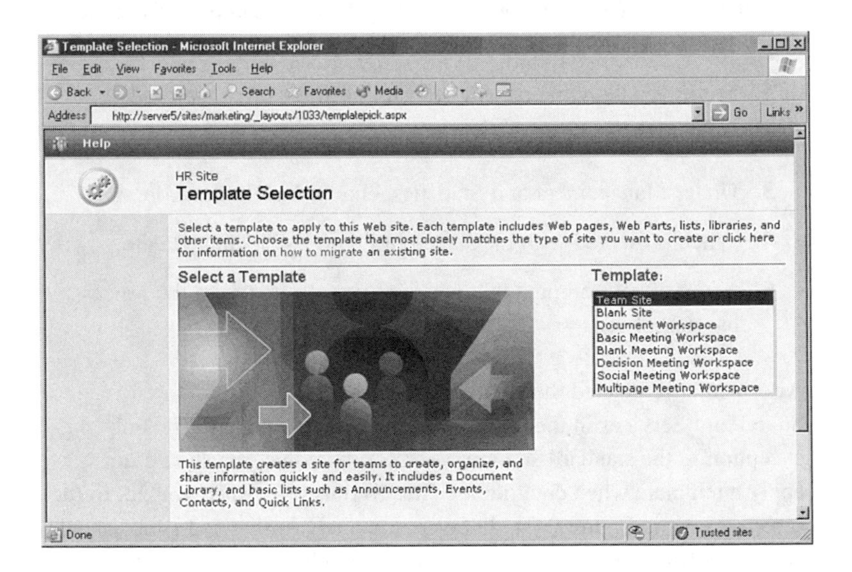

FIGURE 24.4 When re-creating a site to be restored, stop at this screen.

For more information on the specifics of creating a site, reference Lesson 23, "Creating Sites."

Restoring Sites from FrontPage Backups

Once you have deleted the original site and created a new site in the same URL location (but without applying the template), you are ready to restore the site using FrontPage. To perform the restore, do the following:

1. Open Microsoft Office FrontPage 2003.
2. Go to **File**, **Open Site**.
3. In the **Site name** field, enter in the URL of the site you want to restore (for example, http://servername/sites/marketing) and then click **Open**.
4. Authenticate if prompted.
5. Go to **Tools**, **Server**, **Restore Web Site**.
6. Select the .fwp file you created when you backed up the site previously. Click **Open**.
7. Click **OK** when prompted to restore the site, as shown in Figure 24.5.

FIGURE 24.5 Restoring a SharePoint site.

8. The restore process will begin. Click **OK** when it completes.

Backing Up SharePoint Sites with Templates

Another technique for backing up and restoring information in a site is to save the site to a site template and then use that template to create a new site. This technique is convenient because it allows you to restore a site to a new location.

CAUTION The downside to backing up sites using templates is that a Site Template file has a hard limit of 10MB. If your site is larger than 10MB, you will not be able to use this approach.

To back up an existing site to a template so that it can be restored elsewhere, perform the following steps:

1. From the site home page, click **Site Settings** on the top link bar.
2. Under the Administration section, click **Go to Site Administration**.
3. Under Management and Statistics, click **Save site as template**.
4. Enter a filename for the STP file and a title and description for the template file. To fully back up the site, you will also need to select the check box **Include content**, as shown in Figure 24.6.
5. Click **OK** to finish the procedure.

Once you have saved the site as a template, you can use that same template to restore the site to a different location. In addition, you can transfer the STP file to another server running Windows SharePoint Services and restore it to that server. For more information on creating a site from a template, see Lesson 23.

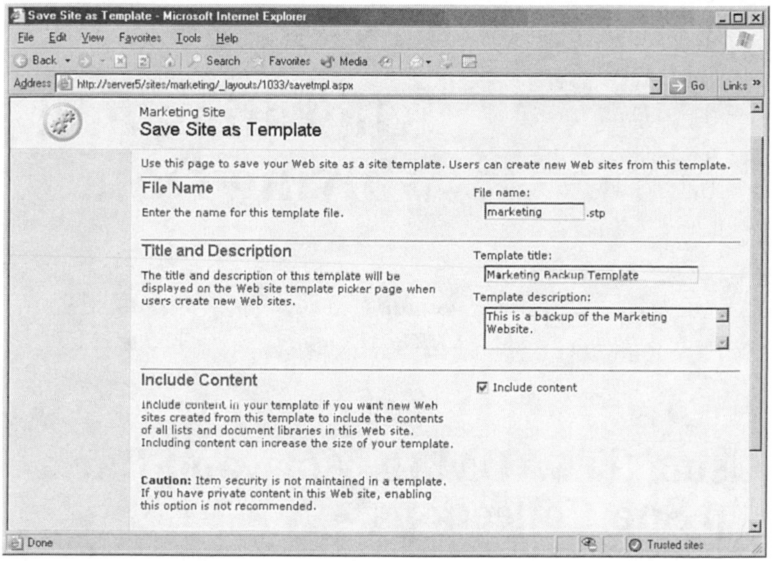

FIGURE 24.6 Backing up a site to a Site Template file.

> **TIP** In addition to the methods described in this chapter, several very good third-party tools are available that provide backup and restore capabilities for individual SharePoint sites or entire site collections. Backup software by Veritas and AvePoint allow for advanced features such as document-level recovery and individual document library backups. It would be wise to examine some of these products as part of a complete SharePoint solution.

Summary

It is critical that you keep your SharePoint site safe and protected from data loss or deletion. Understanding the tools available to back up and restore a site is consequently an important part of this strategy. It is highly recommended that you look at a strategy of backing up your site on a regular basis because it can easily become a business-critical application.

Lesson 25
Migrating and Moving Data

This lesson covers using various utilities such as the STSADM utility to move site collections and the SMIGRATE utility to move and back up sites.

Using STSADM to Move and Back Up Site Collections

The STSADM utility comes installed with Windows SharePoint Services and allows for a great deal of SharePoint functionality. STSADM can import templates, create sites, change settings, and move data. Unlike backing up and moving data with a program such as FrontPage (discussed in Lesson 24, "Backup Strategies"), STSADM must be run from the server on which SharePoint is installed.

> **CAUTION** Take great caution when using the STSADM utility because it can perform a myriad of tasks in SharePoint, such as deleting sites and modifying database information. Be sure to test your data migration in a lab setting before running it against a production environment.

To back up a site collection using STSADM, perform the following steps:

1. From the server that has Windows SharePoint Services installed, open the command prompt by going to **Start**, **Run** and then typing `cmd.exe` into the Open box and click **OK**.

2. Type the following into the command line box:

```
cd \Program files\common files\microsoft shared\web
server extensions\60\bin
```

3. Type in

```
stsadm.exe -o backup -url http://servername/
sitecollectionname
➥ -filename C:\BackupLocation\SiteCollectionBackup.dat
```

Note that `servername` is the name of your server, `sitecollectionname` is the top-level site in a collection, and *c:\BackupLocation* is the directory where you want the backup file to be saved, similar to what is shown in Figure 25.1. Also note that a site collection, although by default appears under the `/sites` virtual directory, can also be at a different level on your SharePoint site.

> **TIP** You have many options available with the STSADM tool. To see these options, type **`stsadm -?`**.

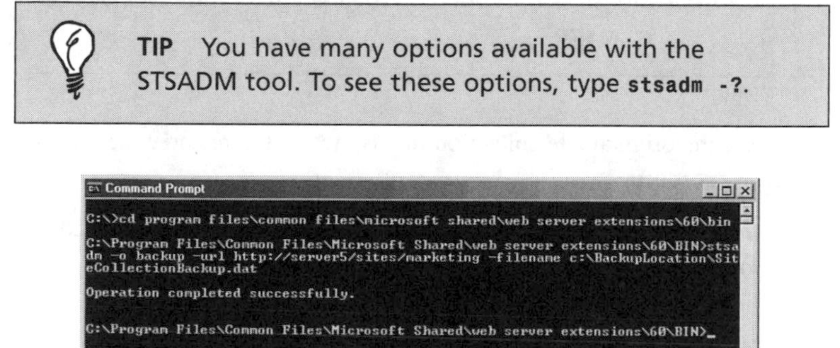

FIGURE 25.1 Backing up a site collection using STSADM.

The advantage in backing up a site collection using this technique is that it can be scripted or run from a batch file.

Deleting a Site Collection in Advance of a STSADM Restore

Using the same STSADM utility, you can restore a site collection to the SharePoint server. To do this, however, either a new SharePoint server must be created (which is what you would do in a disaster recovery scenario) or you have to delete the old site collection. Once the old site collection is deleted, you can restore the original site data. Unlike with FrontPage or SMIGRATE, you don't have to create a blank site to accomplish this, but the site must be deleted; otherwise, the restore will fail.

CAUTION As always, be sure to run these types of operations in a lab environment before testing in production. You can't be assured of the integrity of the backup, so it is important to check it first before deleting your site.

To delete the original site collection in advance of the restore, use the following procedure:

1. From the server that has Windows SharePoint Services installed, open the command prompt by going to **Start**, **Run** and then typing `cmd.exe` in the Open box.
2. Type the following into the command line box:

```
cd \Program files\common files\microsoft shared\web
server extensions\60\bin
```

3. Type in

```
stsadm.exe -o deletesite -url http://servername/
sitecollectionname
```

Note that *`servername`* is the name of the server and *`sitecollectionname`* is the name of your site collection, similar to the example shown in Figure 25.2.

FIGURE 25.2 Deleting a site collection in advance of a restore.

Restoring a SharePoint Site Collection Using the STSADM Utility

Once the original site collection has been deleted, or a new server has been built to replace the old one, you will be ready to restore the site collection using the following procedure:

1. From the server that has Windows SharePoint Services installed, open the command prompt by going to **Start**, **Run** and then typing `cmd.exe` into the Open box.

2. Type the following into the command line box:

```
cd \Program files\common files\microsoft shared\web
server extensions\60\bin
```

3. Type in

```
stsadm.exe -o restore -url http://servername/
sitecollectionname
➥ -filename C:\BackupLocation\SiteCollectionBackup.dat
```

Note that `servername` is the name of your server, `sitecollectionname` is the full path of your site collection (that is, http://servername/sites/marketing), and *C:\BackupLocation* is the location where the backup file was saved to, similar to the example shown in Figure 25.3.

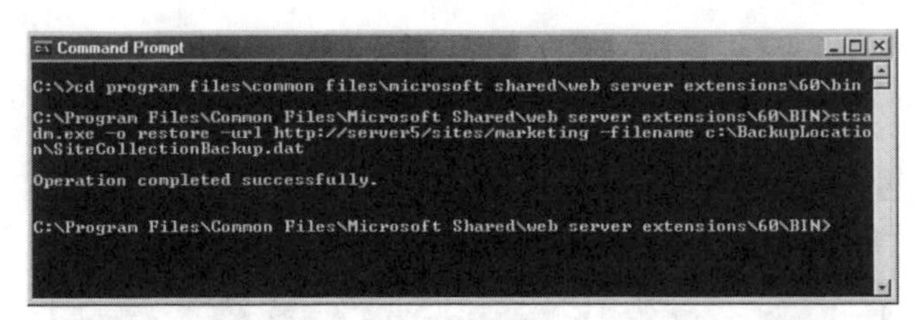

FIGURE 25.3 Restoring a site collection.

Using this approach is ideal for migrating data or restoring a site because it restores all SharePoint site security and SharePoint list data and can be scripted to run via batch files.

Migrating SharePoint Site Data Using the SMIGRATE Utility

SMIGRATE is another utility installed with Windows SharePoint Services that can be used to move or back up data. SMIGRATE was originally designed to migrate data from the older version of Windows SharePoint Services known as *SharePoint Team Services*. Fortunately, it can be used to back up and restore sites as well.

The SMIGRATE utility uses the same mechanism FrontPage uses when backing up sites, except that this version can be scripted to run at specific times because it is a command-line utility.

CAUTION As with backing up a site with FrontPage, SMIGRATE can lose certain security settings on a site, so it is important to validate security settings after performing a restore. For backups and migrations of data without loss of security settings, use the STSADM tool described in the previous section.

The SMIGRATE tool can be used to back up site data or move it by opening a command prompt in the same way described for the STSADM utility and navigating to the same directory (\Program files\common files\microsoft shared\web server extensions\60\bin). Just as with the STSADM utility, the SMIGRATE tool must be run from the SharePoint server. The backup command is as follows:

```
Smigrate.exe -w http://servername/sitecollectionname -f
SiteBackup.fwp
➥ -u AdminName -pw Password4You
```

Here, `AdminName` is the name of a user with admin rights to the site collection and `Password4You` is the password of that user, similar to what is shown in Figure 25.4.

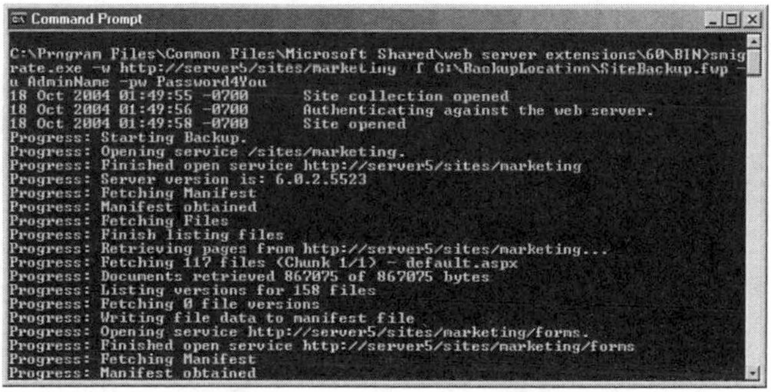

```
Command Prompt
C:\Program Files\Common Files\Microsoft Shared\web server extensions\60\BIN>smig
rate.exe -w http://server5/sites/marketing  f C:\BackupLocation\SiteBackup.fwp -
u AdminName -pw Password4You
18 Oct 2004 01:49:55 -0700      Site collection opened
18 Oct 2004 01:49:56 -0700      Authenticating against the web server.
18 Oct 2004 01:49:58 -0700      Site opened
Progress: Starting Backup.
Progress: Opening service /sites/marketing.
Progress: Finished open service http://server5/sites/marketing
Progress: Server version is: 6.0.2.5523
Progress: Fetching Manifest
Progress: Manifest obtained
Progress: Fetching Files
Progress: Finish listing files
Progress: Retrieving pages from http://server5/sites/marketing...
Progress: Fetching 117 files (Chunk 1/1) - default.aspx
Progress: Documents retrieved 867075 of 867075 bytes
Progress: Listing versions for 158 files
Progress: Fetching 0 file versions
Progress: Writing file data to manifest file
Progress: Opening service http://server5/sites/marketing/forms.
Progress: Finished open service http://server5/sites/marketing/forms
Progress: Fetching Manifest
Progress: Manifest obtained
```

FIGURE 25.4 Backing up a site with the SMIGRATE utility.

As with many of the backup and move utilities, the location where the site collection will be restored must be a blank site, with no template applied. This involves deleting the site and creating a new site, but without applying a site template. Once you have done this, you can restore the site by executing the following command from a command prompt and in the same directory:

```
Smigrate.exe -r -w http://server5/sites/marketing -f C:\
backuplocation\SiteBackup.fwp
➥ -u adminname -pw Password4You
```

Note that `backuplocation` will be the location you specified during the backup process and that the `adminname` and `Password4You` variables are the username and password of a Site Admin, respectively.

Summary

Not only does SharePoint make moving data and backing up sites functional, but it also gives you several different approaches for accomplishing these tasks. Understanding which of these approaches to use for your site should be an important goal of as a Site Administrator.

INDEX

A

B

C

D

E

F

G-H

I-J-K

L

M

N-O

P

Q-R

S

T

U

V

W

X-Y-Z